Dreaming with an AIDS Patient

DREAMING
WITH AN
AIDS PATIENT

ROBERT BOSNAK

SHAMBHALA
Boston & Shaftesbury
1989

Shambhala Publications, Inc.
Horticultural Hall
300 Massachusetts Avenue
Boston, Massachusetts 02115

Shambhala Publications, Inc.
The Old School House
The Courtyard, Bell Street
Shaftesbury, Dorset SP7 8BP

9 8 7 6 5 4 3 2 1
First Edition
Printed in the United States of America on acid-free paper
Distributed in the United States by Random House
and in Canada by Random House of Canada Ltd.
Distributed in the United Kingdom by Element Books Ltd.

Library of Congress Cataloging-in-Publication Data

Bosnak, Robert.
    Dreaming with an AIDS patient / Robert Bosnak.
        p.   cm.
    ISBN 0-87773-502-6
    1. AIDS (Disease)—Psychological aspects. 2. Psychoanalysis—
Case studies. 3. Jung, C. G. (Carl Gustav), 1875-1961. I. Title.
RC607.A26B674 1989   89-42619
362.1'969792—dc20   CIP

Special thanks to

Deanne, Learka, David, Hayao Kawai, Kazuhiko Higuchi,
Marijke Boele van Hensbroek, Jaap Kapteyn,
Dries Langeveld, Herman Vuijsje, Niels van Manen,
Esther Gridazzi Bischoff, Hans van Gerven,
Helmut Kulawik and his staff, Jim Lapierre,
Engelien Heuves-Scholtes, Katsuyuki Ogawa,
Hanako Hamada, Hiromi Watanabe, Jon Lipsky,
David Zoffoli, Kathleen Patrick, Bill Farrier,
Diego Arciniegas, Matt Frederick, Maggie Simpson,
Marshall Hughes, John Hadden, Brent Blair,
and Kendra Crossen.

To you and all who cared for you

Dreaming with an AIDS Patient

1

It is fall. He comes dragging up the stairs to my office. His footstep is tired, like seltzer water gone stale. The knock on the door is without insistence. When I open the door he looks bent. His coat is terribly oversized. It hangs around him like a sack. But he is still elegant—that never leaves him. His clothes are from the days when he had been a robust-looking salesman of expensive fashions.

"Robert, your roses are beautiful," he says. He coughs phlegm into a tissue he carries in his pocket and looks at it with dismay.

"You look pale," I say, concerned.

"I'll get a blood transfusion by the end of the week." He smiles faintly, glad and amused that I noticed. Then, without taking off his coat, he falls into the rocking chair, exhausted. He's one of the first to get the drug AZT, and it wears him out, makes him anemic, but helps keep up his spirits. He is doing something to fight this.

"Your roses out there are beautiful," he repeats. He loves colors and surfaces; that's why he'd gone into fashion. He looks old. We're both late thirties.

I nod and praise my landlord upstairs, who planted the roses some years ago. I love them too. Through the window I had seen Christopher breathe in deep and ponder them, just before starting the effort of ascending my four steps to the front door.

"At least I can climb the stairs to my apartment again. I'm getting stronger." He tilts his head back and stares at the ceiling. Then he closes his eyes for a moment.

"How was your week?" I ask after a while.

"Fine," he lies listlessly. I smile and wait.

▲
_____

Dusk begins to darken the room, and I don't move to turn on the light.

△

He's so different from the jovial man who came to me from Texas less than a year ago.

I hadn't known what to expect when his southern drawl spoke for the first time out of my Cambridge answering machine.

"My name is Christopher P—. I was referred to you by Dr. N—. He told me I should work with you. Please call me back." Followed by a telephone number in Houston.

Damned N. He knows I have no time. And now I have to call Houston. That'll cost a lot of money.

Without any qualms I delay my return call for three days, hoping this Mr. Christopher P. will phone again, saving me the call. I won't be able to take him anyway. I've closed my waiting list. The turnover in analysis is very slow, and I don't see any terminations coming up in the near future.

I call after three days. I'm more intrigued than I had thought by this person phoning all the way from Houston. I hope he won't be home.

"Hi, Dr. Bosnak. Thank you for calling back. Dr. N. gave me your number. I've seen him a few times. I want to move to Boston, and he thinks you'd be best for me."

N. sees all kinds of things in me ever since I worked with a member of his family. I like him, but I don't know what kind of unrealistic expectations he leads his referrals to have. N. specializes in the treatment of gay men. He is straight and he believes that there is an authentic homosexuality that is natural and a neurotic homosexuality that can be therapized away. While my mind circles around N., Mr. P. goes on. He talks rapidly—probably because this is a long-distance call.

"He says I can get rid of my homosexuality. I want out. I don't want this gay life anymore." He sounds very adamant. "I want to work with you in Boston. I'm moving."

N.'s theories echo in my ears. I don't want to think about them.

"I'm sorry," I say honestly. "I won't have an opening for quite a while."

"What's quite a while?"

"Maybe a year," I say tentatively.

"I'll wait," he exclaims cheerfully. "Gives me time to get settled in Boston. I couldn't start right away anyway. I'll first need a job to pay for you."

"It could be a year and a half," I try, pushing him away. I don't really want to work with him. Too complicated. I'm surprised at the immediacy of my resistance.

"I'll wait."

I sigh. What kind of story has that damned N. told about me? I'm annoyed.

△

He calls me after he has moved, to remind me of his existence.

I get an opening in September 1985. He's waited for more than a year.

"Do you grow those roses?" he asks when he comes in. Mr. P. is blond and looks like the epitome of health except that he is slightly overweight. His ruddy face sports a toothy grin, showing an upper jaw that is curved like an asymmetrical beak, making him look outgoing and quickwitted. He must have a vibrant sense of humor. He scratches at some red skin rashes.

"I've had those for years," he exclaims, answering my question. "I've had rashes as long as I can remember."

He gives the cheerful impression of a jovial preacher at Sunday coffee after the church service. A gentle breeze of seriousness blows over his face when he talks about his move up from Houston. He tells me apologetically that he usually dreams a lot but that at this point he only remembers a tiny fragment.

Dream 1

Visit Aunt Lib. I have to cross to the other side.

Since he is clearly distressed that he hasn't brought me more ample dream material, I ask him how important dreams are to him.

"I *love* dreams. In Houston I was part of a dream seminar. We used to draw our dreams. I got a lot out of it. I still make drawings when I have a vivid dream. It makes me feel my spirit. It was the first time since I was kicked out of the seminary that I could feel my soul again. I was going to be a preacher, a fundamentalist preacher."

Then Christopher P. tells me his story.

"My mother was very immature when I was born. She was fifteen and totally incapable of raising me. She was also not interested. My grandparents raised me. To me they were my real parents. They were quite young themselves. With my birth mother I never had any contact. I heard she had one man after the next. Very unhappy love affairs. I don't really know much about that and I don't really care. She never came to our house, and I didn't care to see her."

"What was your home life like?"

"They'd be watching television. Hank would lie slouched on the couch while Ethel was ironing clothes on the dining room table. I always called them by their first names. There wasn't a book in the house besides the Bible. They were very pious. I'm from a strongly fundamentalist background. You know Kentucky?"

"I've been there, but I can't say I know it."

"Kentucky is already the South. Not like the Deep South, but Bible Belt. I loved my grandparents, but I always tried to be away from home. It was so boring there. Ethel was always cleaning up. I couldn't stand it. I always tried to be out of the house." He stares off in the distance.

"What are you thinking of?"

"I'm thinking of Billy. I spent all my time in Billy's house."

"Who's Billy?"

"Billy is the best friend I've ever had. I loved Billy." He pauses for a moment. "I really loved Billy. When we were twelve he was already tall and handsome. His father was the coach of the football team, and Billy was the captain. He was all muscles. But he was so gentle. I always tried to be around him. I think that was the time when I realized that I loved Billy more than anyone. And that I loved boys, not girls. I never was particularly interested in girls. I always was attracted to boys and especially to Billy. Of course I had to be careful not to show it to anyone. You can imagine! With the prejudice against gays I would have been run out of town. Where I come from, 'faggots' are even worse than 'niggers.'

I can hear the quotation marks around the words. There must be a lot of conflict between the inbred prejudices of his childhood and his educated adult self. I wonder what would happen to the analysis if he knew that I am a "kike."

"Billy wasn't gay," Christopher continues, "but he let me touch him. It was the most blissfull time in my life, and I think that since then I've always been looking for him. His body was beautiful. I would have touched him all the time if I'd had the chance. To me he was like God. In church I always mixed him up with Jesus, dreaming of holding him in my arms. I was kind of scrawny and I felt very safe with Billy. He was so beautiful. Of course I couldn't be with Billy too much, or everyone would get suspicious. But since he was always the center of a big crowd, no one noticed that I was always hanging out wherever he was. I would get on my bike and go over to his house. Billy had a motorbike. We would go out on his motorbike and race along the highway." He is silent; I can see a momentary aurora of highways swirl over his head. Then it's gone. "I loved Billy more than I've ever loved anyone."

Love fills the room and we are quietly feeling it.

"How did you get to go to the seminary?" I ask after a while.

He looks at me a bit annoyed because I take him out of his daydreams about Billy. It is just a short flash of irritation, then he begins to explain that he'd always dreamed of being a preacher.

"I've always wanted to be of help to people. I've always

wanted to have something to give—something from my heart; something from my soul. And at that time I wanted to give Jesus to people. Because I loved Jesus. I don't know whether that still had to do with Billy or what it was. I *love* Jesus. I wanted to preach that love to everyone and live a Christian life. So I went to an evangelist Bible college in the South. For three years I was extremely popular. I was head of the student body. I became engaged there to a woman named Ava. I truly loved Ava. We were very intimate friends. She's now living in Los Angeles. I would actually have married her, though my whole sex life with her was one big fake. I touched her and was gentle with her, but I really couldn't bring myself to make love with her. I realized that if I continued with the relationship, my whole life would be based on a lie, and I'd eventually ruin hers too.

"I think it was just after I came back from the Soviet Union, where I'd been with a group of students. I'd love to go back there one day. That was a great trip. It was very interesting to me. For us Christians it was a place they'd always told us horrible stories about. And now I got to really see for myself. That did a lot to my mind. I think it was not long after that trip, that I realized that I didn't want my life to be based on a lie. So I went to Ava and told her that. She was understanding. Of course, she was very upset and we cried a lot together. But she understood. Then I told the college. They kicked me out. They didn't even give me a second hearing. If you're gay you can't be a preacher. They hate gays. They hate faggots."

I can hear the rage at the college and the hatred of faggots in his voice. It is a mixture that seems very volatile to me. The rage at the college could intensify the hatred of faggots, the self-hatred. But I'm most aware of a fury rising within myself. I am furious with the college. I am furious to the point that I see fire in front of my eyes. It is becoming a fury that is going on a rampage. I begin to imagine shooting and killing people. Then I wonder if my fury isn't going beyond all bounds because he is trying to repress it, trying not to feel it. It often happens that if a patient represses emotions that are an integral element of the mood of a memory or image, the emotions come up in me, in the most undifferentiated form. Maybe he doesn't feel the full extent of his rage at the college because it is so mixed in with his self-hatred.

To check my assessment I ask him, "Doesn't that make you furious?"

Suddenly he becomes very "wise" and understanding. He says, "Not really. That's the way they are. I was just like them. I would have kicked me out also. I just had the bad luck that I was who I was."

I don't believe his "wisdom." I don't believe the tone of voice he's talking in. It sounds like someone at peace with himself, but it doesn't correspond with the feeling atmosphere in the room.

I have to check again whether my fury isn't really something of my own that has been touched off. I remember my teenage fears in the locker room that I might be homosexual, at a time when my youthful femininity still looked girlish. I can feel my confusion deeply. It doesn't affect the rage, which erupts like an archaic force. It feels totally elemental, like a building block of the emotional cosmos. Images of Auschwitz, the epitome of rage and destruction in my own universe, arise in my mind. My reaction is out of proportion to the indignation I would personally have about the fact that he was thrown out of the seminary. I feel certain that he is repressing feelings.

"It makes me furious," I hiss.

He looks at me, shy and grateful at the same time. He can feel the fury in me and it has touched him. It somehow feels good to him that I let my anger come up.

"I was devastated. Devastated and rebellious." He sighs and looks depressed. I don't want to pursue the anger right this minute. We are silent. I'm sure we'll get to the rage at some later point.

"So what did you do?" I ask after a while.

"I moved to Florida and became totally promiscuous. I loved any man I thought was beautiful. I had some gorgeous models—guys from the blue jeans ads. I became very popular in the fast gay scene. I drove a convertible, I had beautiful Afghan dogs, dinner on the beach, luxury places, you name it. It was also the beginning of my work in the fashion business. I'm very good at sales. People trust me. I can sell them anything because they sense that I'll never sell them something that doesn't look great on them. . . That fast gay scene, that's the life I want to get out of. I don't want it anymore. I don't want to be gay anymore."

It is close to the end of the hour and I want to get back to the dream, so I ask him, "Who is Aunt Lib?"

"I hardly knew her. I couldn't tell you anything about her. She was some friend of Ethel's. My grandmother. But maybe it has something to do with liberation. Women's lib. Maybe it means that I can be liberated from being gay. Because I have to cross over to another side, to the straight side."

What is this desire to get away from being gay? The mysterious urgency behind it forces the dream into a single optic. All he can see is his desire to leave the gay life. Why? And crossing over to the other side—what's that all about?

I have no idea.

▲

2

Working on dreams is like weaving textures of emotion. Through constant focus on each individual feeling, we intensify the dream, we stew it in its own juices, refining raw feelings in the hope of transforming our emotional selves.

Here follow four dreams from the first month. They have a close affinity because of their common feeling tone, that is, they were told in the same kind of emotional atmosphere. Christopher's account, *exactly* as written down in his brown corduroy dream journal, is followed by his descriptions of the images during the session. (Throughout the book, dreams taken directly from Christopher's book are printed in italic type, while dreams that I have reconstructed from memory are in Roman type.)

When a dreamer describes a dream to me and we begin to work on it, images get etched into my memory. They return when I hear or read the written text of the dream. Since I don't take notes during sessions, I only have Christopher's written accounts of his dreams and my own recollections on which to build a re-creation of our discussions. My descriptions of our sessions are therefore not verbatim accounts but consist of my memory of the way our conversations grew his dream images on my soil.

Dream 2

Dream of driving around something like a lake on a white speed boat. I'm not driving and feel as though I could be thrown off and should possibly take control and drive. We come to a place where we have to go through and a weasel of a small wiry man charges us to go through. It is some sort of passage, but not a lock. I paid it but remember feeling he charged too much (embezzled me) and feared I would not have enough for later.

"We're on this boat. I don't remember who I'm with. It's white. The lake is calm but we're going very fast. It feels out of control. I sit on the side and feel the wind in my hair. It feels scary and terrific at the same time. It's in the afternoon. Blue skies. Then we come to this passage. Somehow the boat stops and I see this little weasel guy, this creep asking us for money. He gives me the creeps. I get goose bumps. I don't want to pay. I know that he is charging way too much. But we have to get through to get to the other body of water. It's something like two lakes that are connected. We have to get to the other lake. He rips me off. I pay, but I feel totally ripped off. I count my money, and I don't think I'll have enough at the next passage. I'm scared."

Dream 3

Dream of being at some sort of dinner or coronation of a woman at which a beautiful garment is carried around elevated in the air and placed on her. It is gold, turquoise and light.

"It's like a cape made of light, and at first it seems to me that it's actually floating through the air. Then I see that it's lifted through the air by people who carry it up to her. It is evening. The garment is so light that it can almost float by itself, like a veil. The dinner takes place outside, or in some very large hall. I feel elated and very pleased that I was invited. Everyone around is very joyous for the occasion. It is very important. The queen is dressed in dark clothes. But I can't remember her face. She walks very elegantly. I'm impressed by her. She is my queen. The queen of my country."

Dream 4

Dream of walking up a hill in some sort of

procession. I later realize that it is a wedding and I am the groom. It seems that there is a problem with being one rose short for the attendants, and to give her one of the flowers I brought would be odd because they are different from the roses—like a real long cockscomb.

"It is a slow procession. I remember mainly women. The attendants were all women. I had the other flower. I don't know if that was because I was the groom. I'm going to marry her. But I don't know her. At first I don't even know that I'm the groom. It's dark. In the end I'm confused because I don't know what to do about the flowers, and I'm somehow responsible for them. I never get to see my bride. At some point the hill is steep. It feels like a ritual procession. We weren't wearing regular clothes. I don't remember what we had on, though. The attendants were dressed in light colors."

Dream 5

Dream occurring in the basement of a modern structure—house-bar or club. People are seated at hemispherical counter which I view from the back. My focus is on a woman at this counter. She has on a magenta wool suit and a gold pendant in the back. It is three fish (like angelfish). Hence she is "fish-woman" and I become very protective of her knowing or intuiting that she is pregnant. (Later I recognize with my child—who would be fish child)

"I remember walking down these wide marble stairs in this modern building. I'm dressed casually. I'm going to the bar to get a drink. But the building is not a hotel or a restaurant. It is more like a fashionable apartment house or office building. When I come down the marble stairs, one hand in my pocket, I see this woman in the magenta sweater. She is sitting between several other people, but my focus is only on her. I feel that she is somehow related to me in a very special way. I come closer and see the golden angelfish pendant hanging on

the magenta back of her sweater. I never see her face. But the
fish on the back are shining and gold and I stare long and
intently at them. This conveys to me in some way that she is
the pregnant fishwoman. I immediately want to take care of
her, see to it that no harm comes to her. I look at the fish
again. She doesn't turn around. Then I realize that she is
pregnant with my baby. My own fishchild. I'm very moved. I
think I almost cry, and I want to see her face but I wake up."

△

The second dream, about the white speedboat, repeats the
theme of going to the other side. I'm puzzled. The first two
dreams seem to insist on a crossing. Christopher happily
connects it again to his desire to leave the gay world, and I am
again surprised at the force with which he presents this wish.
I ask him if there are any other crossings he can think of, but
he draws a blank.

The little weasel makes me squirm. I always feel that I
charge too much for analysis. I feel a compulsion to tell you,
reader, that I charge less than most analysts, which proves
my discomfort. I blush when I tell him of my distress. He
laughs and answers that it hadn't occurred to him, which
doesn't prove anything nor does it decrease my discomfort.
With some effort I tell myself that I am getting trapped in a
trait of my own, making me unable to look at the dream. I am
able to give my "analyst as rip off artist" a seat somewhere
else in the room and look together with Christopher at the
little fellow.

"He jumps up and down. He wants attention. He has to be
paid, otherwise I'll have to hang around on this lake forever,"
says Christopher.

"And then you wouldn't be going anywhere," I add.

He nods. "I feel stuck on that lake."

"In your white speedboat going out of control."

He looks puzzled. "What do you mean?"

"There doesn't seem to be any direction to your speed. It's
life in the fast lane with no one at the wheel. Sounds

precarious to me. Especially if you can't get out to other waters."

While he ponders this I drift off in the direction of the practicum in alchemy and dreams that I teach each fall at the C. G. Jung Institute in Boston. The whiteness of the speedboat reminds me of a section I've just taught on the virginal white, a condition of youthful innocence and trust that is naturally optimistic and unhampered by insight. In alchemy this state is often a prelude to a darkening, when the motherly white cream turns sour and rots, giving rise to consciousness. The way in which the innocent white begins to rot is through the emergence of ambiguity. Things don't seem certain anymore, and the world is no longer a safe place. Suddenly events have a multiplicity of meanings, and the clear direction is lost as the hitherto unquestioned worldview falls apart. Alchemy attributes this transformation to an admixture of mercury, the fluid silver, a metal of inherent contradiction, destroying the single-minded certainty of virginity. Mercury is the crafty, tricky god of thieves, and one of his favorite animals, besides the fox, is the weasel who robs the coop. He trips up our innocence and makes us tumble into the night. He can be as small as your pinky and continuously shifts his shape. Mercury is the guide in the great transformation—death—leading the souls of the dead to the netherworld, helping them cross to the other side. For all these reasons he is the patron god of the psychoanalytic profession, and my character trait of being a rip-off artist belongs to his realm. I see the little weasel man cast a foul grin. I'd better watch out.

Christopher can't stand queens. When he sees one enter a gay bar he always says, "Look at her. Get me out of here." Effeminacy makes him sick. Judging by the coronation of the queen in dream 3, it seems that woman is a very elevated creature. Her garment is light as a feather, almost floating, almost weightless, almost a pure, disembodied image woven of light. She is out of this world. Christopher is her subject. Woman is immensely powerful, ruling his world. In dream 4 he becomes her consort. His relationship to woman seems fairytalelike. "Women have been very good to me," he says. "I have a close woman friend back in Houston. She says that I could come back there any time and live with her. At another point a woman friend paid for part of my school." It seems that he has a filial relationship to women who take care of him. These women are considerably older than he, very loving, caring, and Christian. They are the mainstays of the Christian communities he has belonged to. None of his primary relationships, however, are with women. His emotions, passions, and sufferings are over men. Intimate struggle brings an archaic image down into human flesh. Woman can remain elevated if contact with her is limited to caring, spiritual, Christian love. Woman and Madonna are synonymous in dream 5. She is going to give birth to the fish child, and Jesus has long been called ICHTHYS, the Greek word for "fish" and an ancient acronym meaning "Jesus Christ Son of God and Savior."

It is hard for me at this time not to get irritated at his Christianity. It is the cruel core of his self-disgust as well as the supreme center of all value to him. And my relationship to his fundamental paradox is one of attraction and repulsion simultaneously.

I'm reminded as well of the image of marriage in alchemy. Alchemists imagined the fusion of different metals into an alloy, a new metal, as a divine marriage, where the king and the queen dissolved together in a dark stream of images. They were reconstituted as a new being, a man-woman, a hermaphrodite, partaking of both sun and moon, gold and silver, the ultimate alloy. The process the alchemists describe shows marriage as an ever more intensified struggle of opposing forces held together in a painful paradox. This warring love leads to dissolution, in which the opposing forces fall apart and get a chance to reconstitute in a new form. At one point, when the marital struggle has reached a point of frenzy—when the full force of the joint family neurosis has hit like a bomb—all that remains is the sense of burned-outness and death. From all this darkness a new capacity for relationship emerges, hardened like a metal that has been switched time and again back and forth between the fire and the ice-cold water. No living happily ever after for the alchemists!

Looking at Christopher's dreams from a spatial point of view, I see first two horizontal motions, or crossings, followed by two vertical motions, the procession up the hill and the walk down the stairs. These are movements in all directions of three-dimensional space. A state of transit seems to be constellated, moving from one location to another, one state to another. This is a dreamscape of undertows in all directions.

3

"I've had this itch since I was a baby," he says, taking a tissue and spitting into it. He stares thoughtfully at the mucus.

"A cold?" I ask, looking at the red blotches on his skin. Some of them look scratched. "That looks like a nasty rash," I add.

"Not really. It's not too bad. Just irritating once in a while." It looks a lot more irritating than his tone of voice conveys. His lightheartedness grates my soul to the point that I'd like to scratch myself. I know we're overlooking something, but I have no idea what.

Dream 6

Dream of me and a young male companion on a high place with some sort of gear on. Perhaps parachute gear. We jump off and float to the bottom but no chutes are used. I remark at his courage to jump so readily his first time. He said I did too, but I said it was not my first time and I was more used to it.

"It was a teenage kid. No, not a lover. More like thirteen, fourteen. He looked very innocent, and I felt very adult next to him. That's why I praised him and why when he praised me, I couldn't take it in because I wanted to be the experienced older man." He looks proud for an instant, then continues, making fun of his own self-importance: "Silly. Very silly. Of course I had never jumped before. I've never jumped with or without a parachute.... It was very pleasant. We floated like we were hanging from a balloon. It was a long ways down. Like the Grand Canyon. Down below was a river. A hell of a long way down. But we landed safely. I wasn't surprised. I never felt in danger."

"How does the floating feel?" I ask, curious.

"A little like deep sea diving, but entirely different."

I nod, because I can feel his description. It feels accurate. "Lighter," I say, "less pressure."

"Exactly," he agrees.

"Feels wonderful," I add, feeling afloat in near-weightlessness. I am reminded of the almost weightless veil of the queen. It seems as if we're falling right into that image. I have little orientation about up or down. I'm disoriented.

"Is it disorienting when you float down?" I ask.

He shakes his head. "It doesn't frighten me."

I decide to mentally store away my feeling of disorientation in the file "Keep an eye out." It corresponds to my disorienting sense that we are overlooking something vital.

"Is the young boy in any way like Billy or Laurence?" I want to know.

"Not like Billy," he answers immediately.

"Isn't Laurence fifteen years younger than you?"

Christopher blushes. "He is a very beautiful boy. I was some kind of a teacher for him. Yes, he does look like Laurence. But much younger than I ever knew Laurence." I can see how attached he still is to Laurence.

He has told me that the decisive reason for moving from Houston to Boston was that Laurence, Christopher's twenty-two-year-old lover, wanted to break up with him. Not that their love had lessened, but Laurence had become restless, wanting more experience.

"Do you miss Laurence?" I ask softly.

He nods. "Sometimes. I miss him and my community there. I felt that I really belonged when I was with my Christian community in Houston. But when I broke up with Laurence I didn't want to go back to the bar scene. I wanted out."

"If you were with Laurence now, would you still want to leave the gay life?" I feel immediately that this is a stupid, hypothetical question that can only hurt. It could easily be taken as a put-down of his desire to leave the gay world.

"I don't know how to answer that," he mutters, confused. I want to change the subject.

"You were Laurence's teacher?"

"In some ways. Laurence was always very optimistic. He had no idea of the shadow side of things. I was older and had more experience."

"So you go down with your optimistic boy, don't you?" I muse.

"I guess so," he says, paying no attention. "Yes, I do miss Laurence. I miss him a lot. He was the first person since Billy that I loved that much. I liked it that I was older than him. I introduced him to religion. His parents were terrible when he told them he was gay. I was with him then. I don't understand those people. I've never met a gentler soul than Laurence. I took care of him. I spoke about the life of the spirit. He had never thought about it. I could give him that." Christopher is silent. Then he shakes his head. "But I'm very happy that I left Houston. Maggie—Margaret of my Christian community—called me again yesterday and said I could come back anytime and live with her. And I do love her. I would also want to be close to Laurence again. But I'm glad I'm here in Boston. It's a little cold, though. Emotionally, I mean. People don't get involved with each other. There's no community like I had down there. And the church here is boring. None of the charismatic communities I like."

"There's a charismatic black community two blocks from here. They certainly sound very alive," I say, aware of his probable response.

He just smiles and nods.

"So why are you glad that you are here in Boston?" I ask.

"There's more going on in Boston. And a job like this I could never get in Houston. Houston is not doing too hot. Lots of houses for sale. People leaving. Here I have a job that gets me more than twice what I'd gotten elsewhere. I also like the gay community here. They've been very helpful. And I like the fact that all these schools are here. I'd like to go back to school, learn more about psychology. And dreams."

Dream 7

Dream of going in "my" school and am very disoriented for some reason. Have difficulty getting to my locker (where I'm trying to get aspirin for a headache). End up on the wrong floor twice and can't remember combination.

"I've never been to that building before. It's like a warehouse with warehouse elevators. It's my school. My high school, I think. It had lockers. But it wasn't the high school I really went to. I walk around like a zombie who doesn't know his way around. Everything is very slow and confusing. When I'm on the wrong floor for the fourth time, I get irritated. My headache just keeps getting worse. It comes up from between my eyes. Piercing. I keep stumbling around looking for the aspirin."

"Do you often get headaches?"

"Hardly ever. I always take aspirin when I do have one."

"Are the headaches you do have similar to the dream headache?"

"This is sharper. More penetrating. It goes into my skull."

"Does it feel as if there is a connection between your feeling of disorientation and the headache?" It seems obvious to me, but I ask anyway.

"I don't think so. I have the headache before I get disoriented."

I'm skeptical. I believe that the headache is the physical counterpart of the mental disorientation. But I don't insist. So I ask:

"Can you describe one of the floors to me?"

"It's brown and dark like a warehouse. I can see all the exposed wood. There are few other people around. In fact, I can't remember anyone. I'm just looking. The lockers are made of metal. They're somewhere in the back of the hallway. I always seem to keep aspirin in there. I'm wearing sneakers. I'm about my present age. But I'm also going to high school. There are metal beams in the ceiling."

"Can you try to feel the disorientation when you can't find the lockers?" I ask softly and with caution. This is a therapeutic move that shouldn't create resistance. It doesn't. He closes his eyes and in memory is back in the warehouse-like high school.

"I can see myself running around inside the school. I'm moving slowly, but it's as if I'm running at the same time. I've no idea where I'm going. Sometimes I can visualize the lockers, but I don't know where they are. And sometimes I know where they are, and then I forget. In the elevator I get confused. That's when it starts. In the elevator I get very confused and disoriented. I don't know what floor I'm on or what floor I'm going to. Yes, now I can feel it. There it is again. I feel very disoriented. I have no idea where I'm going."

"You don't know whether you're coming or going," I interject under my breath, noting to myself that the confusion begins in the elevator and comparing it to my feeling of disorientation when he floated down in dream 6. Fortunately he doesn't hear me.

"It almost makes me dizzy. I can't find where I am. Now that headache is coming back."

"Concentrate on the headache."

"It begins between my eyes. It's very sharp. I just want to get rid of it. I just want it to go away."

Dream 8

In another "underground scene" two younger women enter the room from a hallway and I'm engaged in a scene like we're in a play but I don't know my lines and can't find my place when looking thru the script.

"This is different from the underground scene at the bar. It's more like a cellar under something. The hallway has pipes on the ceiling. Beige colors. And I'm in some kind of underground auditorium. I remember that the ones coming in were girls, but I don't remember much about them. They were young—high school age, I'd say. I'm on a stage. Reading through a script. I'm trying desperately to find my lines. I have no idea what they are."

"Have you ever had dreams like that before, where you don't know your cue?"

"No. But I've heard people tell those dreams. They're pretty common, aren't they?"

"It just strikes me that it comes just after that dream about disorientation. What does it feel like when you can't find your place in the script?"

"I feel all kinds of pressure. From the others on the stage, from the girls who come in. I feel like a fool. I don't even know who I'm supposed to be in the play. I don't know anything. I'm very confused."

"Concentrate on the confusion."

"I don't know who I am anymore. I don't have a clue. I hate this. I'm so embarrassed. I'm terribly embarrassed."

"Have you ever felt like this?"

"I can't remember. I feels like I don't know who I am. I've never experienced that. I never lost my sense of who I was. Not even when they kicked me out of the seminary."

The mood he conveys, the feeling of loss of identity, goes directly against everything he is consciously feeling at the moment. He has a strong sense of who he is. Even though he's convinced that he doesn't want to be gay anymore, that fact itself doesn't confuse him. He feels secure in his profession. He knows who he is. I mention this and we puzzle over the contradiction, but we don't get anywhere.

Dream 9

Dream of riding bicycle down slippery way with some steps here and there—like wooden decking; ride up to and into house. Embarrassed to bring bike into strangers' house—though I'm no stranger there. Hear vehicle zoom up to area below house (it's on a hill). Is high powered car. It takes off toward the

*shore. I had the feeling he was there to meet me and
went on without me, but I enjoyed walking in a
leisurely way toward the shore which I could see over
the rolling sandy plains but the surf was very loud, to
which I remarked.*

"I used to ride my bicycle to Billy's house. But this was
different. I'm my present age. I can't remember much of this
dream. I remember my embarrassment when I'm suddenly in
these people's living room with my bicycle, but I mainly
remember the roar of the waves. It is much, much louder
than usual."

"What does the living room look like?"

"I don't remember. I just remember my embarrassment."

"How do you know these people?"

"No idea. But I know them. Not very well. Not well
enough to ride my bike into their living room." He smiles. "I
also remember the roar of the engines. It's a powerful car—
some kind of racing car. It may be a lover who is picking me
up. Or some friends. I'm not annoyed that they don't wait for
me. I walk leisurely down the hill. Then comes the sound of
the ocean. But there is no storm going on."

"Can you still hear those waves?"

He nods emphatically. "I can hear them roar right in my
ears. It is very unusual to hear them over such distance. The
ocean seems to be wild on a clear day. Very wild. Menacing."

"Does it frighten you?"

"No, but it's eerie somehow. As if the ocean were pouncing
the shoreline."

"Like when you hear the blood rush in your ears when your
heart beats fast?" He looks blank at this remark. Still, I can
feel my blood rushing and my heart beat with apprehension.
We're coming close to the sea of action. The unknown is
pounding the shores of his conscious world. The slippery
movement down seems to lead to the ocean, the motions and
moods of pouncing passion.

"How is your love life at the moment?"

"Not very interesting. I'm living with John, but we aren't

lovers. He's the most important person in my life now. We're doing very well together. I sometimes pick up a guy. I have no trouble picking up guys. But sex isn't a high anymore. It's not intimate either. In Florida we sometimes took poppers when we had sex. That was wild. But now there's no wild sex in my life. I can't complain. But I miss the intimacy I had with Laurence. Laurence was here last week with his new lover, who's twenty-five. I lent them my convertible to drive to the Cape. I'm not even jealous," he adds, expecting my question. His voice sounds forced.

"Could that be the car that went on without you in the dream?"

"Yes, it could be," he answers, blushing. "Maybe I did feel left out."

We sit silently for a moment. I can see how much he loves Laurence and how much he is trying to give Laurence his freedom.

"Can you concentrate on the sound of the ocean again."

He closes his eyes.

"Does it sound as if the ocean is attacking the shore?"

"That's exactly what it sounds like."

△

Christopher never presented the following dream in analysis. It remained like a silent orphan in his brown corduroy dream book until he let me photocopy the entire book. So we never got to talk about it.

Dream 10

Dream of food—placing unwrapped raw hamburger behind tire of van. Take clams on half-shell out of shoe. Later dream of almost tasting dessert. Unravel it as an old woman says, if I don't like her, don't stay for dessert. Lie down with Ava—ask if she is comfortable. She pats me on the back. My roommate is tearing up peach nightshirt, for which I chide him. Back to the "Christmas room" where the dessert

*was. I am fiddling with some contraption I can't get
to work. Am embarrassed because I think it is
probably pretty simple. On my arm is a bracelet with
hooks on it, reminding me of the cockscomb bloom of
the other dream. I think they might think it is
effeminate but disregard it. I show others how it
works. Each hook becomes a teddy bear that will hold
on to the others.*

Let us try to approach these hieroglyphics by coaxing the
images into figures of speech. Then we can ruminate over
each individual scene, imagining it carefully and in as much
detail as we can muster, as if it were an image of our own.

This is a tale of food. About our world of nutrition. It is
about how we nurture ourselves.

Something raw is becoming unwrapped. Something is
coming out in the open. It is placed, as if it were the casualty
from an accident, behind the van, the vehicle that lugs our
stuff around; the modern-day beast of burden. Flesh gone
through a meat grinder feels raw and hurts.

In this state, we meat (accidental typo) the clam on the
half-shell, Venus, the oceanic vulva. The Love Goddess was
born from the froth of the waters, the half-shell underfoot. In
our tale she comes from the shoe, the world of our stand-
point. Here we make a stand, saying "I am I." The shoe is also
the place of connection between us and what we are basically
not, between ourselves and the outside world. Here our
gravity meets the ground that carries us through the medium
of the shoe, the manmade interface with this world underfoot. Here we dream of the erotic relations between self and
other.

The main course is over. We almost get to taste the
sweetness of dessert (called "afterdish" in German). We
unravel toward the after-food.

"If you don't like me, don't stay for dessert," says the old
woman. If we don't like archaic feminity, we won't taste the
sweetness that could be our desert (spelling intentional) and
will miss the icing on the cake.

"So I lay down with woman," says a Christopher in my imagination, "my fiancée, the woman who engaged me most. My female counterpart is at peace with me, patting my back in encouragement, while my male counterpart attacks the peachy night-skin. He is the one who always tears my peachy softness to pieces because he can't stand it. I disapprove." The movement reverses once more. It went from raw grind through vulva almost to sweet aftertaste; spurned woman of old gives way to gently engaging with woman. But man cannot stand it and tears the peachiness to pieces, bending the direction away from woman once again. It seems that one pivot of motion is Christopher's masculine intolerance of soft-skinned nocturnal femininity.

The state of dessert, sweet afterdish, is celebrated in the land of Christmas, the birth of the Fish, the feast of childhood. Here, in the land of the Infant, my contraption won't work. My contraption just won't spring to action. I'm sure everyone else knows how to handle his tool, but I don't know what to do with mine. I'm embarrassed, impotent.

On my arm, accentuating my pulse and hand, I'm hooked by the bracelet of the cockscomb. The hook is the cock, not the rose of the female attendants. Hooked on cock. I hear "them" think this effeminate; they think I'm a queen. I feel paranoid, but disregard it. I know how this one works. The potentially effeminate bracelet I can handle, in contradistinction to my tool I couldn't get to work.

The more I show my cock-hooks, the more my bloom turns into a cuddly teddy. The cuddly bear that holds on to the other cuddly bear. The dependent chain of childhood surrounds the pulse of my life.

4

"I've been fired!" He's grinning as though he couldn't care less.

"I'll find something else," he insists with pride, as if luxury jobs in fashion sales are a dime a dozen. I feel very uncomfortable, the way I always feel when he's obviously deluding himself. He becomes jovial and happy-go-lucky.

"But doesn't it piss you off?" I ask, incredulous.

"Of course!" he exclaims. "How the hell could they think that I'd risk a forty-five-thousand-dollar-a-year job for eighteen bucks? Do they think I'm dumb?"

He'd been fired by the fancy store because he made a certain booking on a Sunday, which gave him an eighteen-dollar advantage in his commission.

"I'd asked my boss several times if I could book refunds on returned weekday merchandise to Sunday, and she had answered yes every time. So last Sunday I do it and they fire me. She tells me that I booked it to Sunday on purpose to get the extra eighteen dollars' commission. She called it fraud. That's absurd! But I have no recourse. They believe her." Finally he looks mad. It is fifty minutes into the sixty-minute session. He had talked the first forty minutes about irrelevant things before he volunteered the information that he'd been fired. He must be very ashamed, so that he hardly dared tell me. But we don't penetrate the feelings of shame and loss. Anger is as far as we get.

I feel the same burning humiliation and impotent rage as when he told me about his expulsion from the seminary. I can smell dark thunder gathering, but I can't get through to him.

After the short anger he's sunny again. "I'll find something else, that's for sure."

His defiance reverberates after he has left. I feel very apprehensive.

△

He doesn't turn up for his next session one week later. Ten minutes into the hour I feel a short spurt of panic. The Jewish mother inside me cries that he might have killed himself. I try to soothe her, but she is all pale and convinced. It is one of those intuitive certainties that won't go away. I call Christopher. Nobody home. "You see?" my "mother" screams, overcome by anxious worry—"He's dead!" I can feel hysterical fear surge through my veins. I yell at her to shut up, but the anxiety persists. "He probably just forgot," I insist feebly.

At night I call again. No answer. Now my hysteria has a field day. I wonder what makes me so anxious.

He doesn't show up the next session either. Why would he leave after being so eager to start analysis? I notice that I don't even feel rejected. Usually I feel rejected when people stay away without telling me why.

I call his house. To my relief, John, Christopher's roommate, answers.

"Christopher had to go to Houston suddenly to take care of some business. He won't be back for a few weeks." John sounds friendly and tired. I like him instantly. I hang up and note that I haven't asked for a Houston phone number. "See!" I tell my maternal hysteria. But it doesn't calm her. She reminds me of this one patient I had who returned to his home far away to kill himself. "You can shove your doomsday," I mutter, nervously pacing my office.

△

After my first afternoon session the next day I find a message on my answering machine, whispered by dying lungs. I can hardly make out the telephone number. I call immediately.

"Hello, Robert Bosnak," the voice answers, gasping for air.

"I have pneumocystis." When I don't react, he adds, "I have AIDS."

The bomb explodes. I can hardly hear him when he asks me to call him tomorrow morning because he needs to tell me a dream. After he hangs up, I sit with the receiver in my hand, staring into empty space.

We have never talked about AIDS, even though Houston is one of the hotbeds of the disease. We must both have been terribly resistant against considering it. Suddenly all the resistances come into focus. My desire not to take him, in the beginning, postponing the analysis as long as ethically possible; his mysterious urgency to leave the gay world; his need to stay away from his feelings. AIDS casts a long and frightening shadow ahead. His initial dream—"I have to cross to the other side"—now shines in an altogether different light. I feel a sudden pang of loss and weep as I hang up.

I call him Saturday morning, looking out over the brilliant snow in my backyard. The landscape looks exquisite and frail. His voice is barely more than a gasp. I have trouble hearing each word.

Dream 11

First I remember a voice saying, "O my God, he's pulled it out.' I awake in a large medical hospital-looking room. There are two long windows, a door on the left-hand side. I'm lying on an old metal hospital bed. Behind me lies a mid-complected person, maybe Italian, in any case darker than me. Behind each of us there is a twenty-inch-tall rubbery wet and cartilagelike vital organ in the shape of a figure 8 we had pulled out of ourselves. At the head of the bed there were bottles with blood, with one line going to him and one to me. Both lines went over to "Her" [in his later written account he writes it this way]. *The room was divided in two with a diagonal line. On the other side of the room where*

▲
---

*the blood lines lead to was a picture of Marilyn
Monroe surrounded by a marquee with little lights,
like to announce the star. If I turned the valve in the
right way on the blood line, either she or I would die.
If I did it right she would die. I wanted very much to
live and she doesn't care much about life since she has
killed herself already. I mess with the valves because I
want to live. Her side of the room was dark like
night. The man behind me looked almost dead.*

I see the dream happening while he is talking to me. At the
same time I notice my own images. I imagine how he has
pulled his immune system, in the shape of eternity, out of his
body. Especially at the name Marilyn Monroe I get distracted,
knowing that my entire study is filled with pictures of her,
remembering how she has forever been my Love Goddess,
portraying to me as a young Dutch boy the seduction of
distant America. I see my wife looking at me intently from
the kitchen, noticing the tears rolling down my cheeks, and I
realize that Christopher's AIDS is going to bring the disease
close to my whole family, out of newspaper unreality into the
kitchen. I feel the survival force rear its head. Christopher
must be kept alive. We'll fight and win over this so-called
invincible scourge.

"Do you believe that you can put that piece of cartilage
back in?" I hear myself ask after a silence. My fighting spirit
is already thinking of ways to lick this illness.

"No idea," he responds listlessly. "It could have to do with
one of the tubes going down to my lungs that I tried to pull
out when I was in the coma. They told me afterward that I
had tried to pull it out. I don't know if that was a dream or a
real nurse coming in," he adds, nearly suffocating in this long
sentence. "My hands are tied to the bed now," he whispers
almost inaudibly. I can feel him like a captured animal
withering away in a trap. "They say I'll be out in two weeks.
They're very good to me here. I have a blind friend who came
every day during my coma." I can hear him sob. "I have to go
now."

29

"I'll see you in two weeks," I say.

"I'll take a taxi as soon as I can."

As I stare at the cold winter out in back, my wife asks me if it is bad. "Very bad," I mumble, not understanding why I am sure that I shouldn't run over to the hospital right away.

△

In the next few days I observe my conviction grow that Christopher is not going to die. I realize with overwhelming certainty that Christopher has never had this disease before and that the chances medicine talks about are exclusively statistical and have nothing to do with Christopher as an individual. The conviction grows as a plant grows, on its own, generating its own energy, producing more power as it grows larger, consuming me. I grow increasingly furious with the medical profession for convincing people that AIDS is as deadly as a meat grinder. The optimism I feel is irresistible; it takes me over.

Now I understand why we've never talked about AIDS. This passionate optimism must have been going on in him for much longer. It belongs to the dawn of the disease, in the same way a seizure casts an aura before it. It is the life force gathering momentum to survive this crossing. It is the resistance against death. I realize that now I am driven by this potent force. I feel some manic giddiness as well, singing songs of the Great Healer. I can do nothing but let myself be pulled out to sea by the riptide and identify totally with the survival force.

△

I am waiting for his arrival at my Cambridge office on a January afternoon. My neighbors have just dug themselves out of the latest storm, and the street shimmers with sunlight when the car of the woman from the AIDS Action Committee pulls up. Since Christopher lost his job before the onset of the illness, he has no insurance and no income but welfare. Taxis are out of his reach. The AIDS Action Committee responds promptly and provides transport between his home and my office.

He's exhausted when he shuffles into my room. The four steps to my front door have worn him out totally. He is a skeleton in a down jacket. His long fingers are bluish. Without taking off his coat, he plops down in the rocker, fragile as a glass figurine.

"Is it too cold for you here?" I ask, worried.

He nods, rubbing his hands together. I jump up and in one quick motion grab the electric heater, put it in front of him, and turn it up full blast. I'm ashamed of my agility.

"I can hardly get up the stairs to my house. I have to rest every few steps. This is my first time out since the hospital. I don't dare go anywhere, because I'm not sure whether I'll make it back up the stairs. Tonight John is specially coming home early from work to help me up the stairs." He looks ashamed that he has to bother people. He has always been ferociously independent.

"And I can't come to see you anymore. I don't have any money, no insurance, nothing." He looks down, sad beyond tears.

"Of course we'll continue," I say quickly. "Once in analysis, always in analysis."

"But I can't pay you," he insists.

"We'll find something," I add, so he won't feel guilty. "You can pay me when you have a job again."

He looks at me, sad, not sure whether he'll ever have a job again.

"I would like it if you kept seeing me," I emphasize.

He looks at me, grateful. He clearly wants very much to continue seeing me. I have to be careful not to make him feel our relationship as a one-way street. I have to show him that I get as much from our meetings as he. Gratitude can kill analysis. It first obscures negative feelings toward the analyst and then generates random hostility from the accumulated guilt.

"Here's the dream I told you," he says, handing me an

almost illegible written version. It is hard to believe that this is the same robust man with bold handwriting I saw a month ago. He looks pleased that he's able to give me something. His dreams are his payment.

"I had two other dreams, but I didn't have the energy to write them down," he whispers. Talking is wearing him out. At the same time he wants to do as much work as he can during this hour. He's pushing himself. At this point my respect for him takes root, only to grow in the following months. I wait till he catches his breath.

Dream 12

There's a woman holding an infant on the bank of the river. I'm floating down the river and she pulls me out. Suddenly I am the baby in her arms. I feel safe.

Dream 13

The river is very fast. It is white water. Whirlpools everywhere. I see some boys being pulled downstream. They are sucked into the whirlpool and disappear. Then I see them struggling their way back to the surface. They make it but they are exhausted.

He stops, utterly worn out by the telling of these two dreams.

"What does the woman in the first dream look like?" I ask after a while.

"I don't really remember," he says, drained.

"Just try," I gently push.

"Well, I remember her wearing some kind of long skirt, like those hippies used to wear. She's some kind of earth mother. You know, those women who are pregnant all the time and are always doing something with a child hanging on to them." He smiles.

"Is she pregnant now?"

"I don't believe so."

"Do you remember what it felt like to be her baby?"

"It was wonderful. It made me feel all relaxed."

"Can you feel it now?"

He closed his eyes and leans back in the rocker.

"What do you feel?" I ask him after I've given him time to get submerged in the feeling.

"I'm becoming all rosy. I feel very warm and very supported. As if I can just fall asleep and everything will be wonderful when I wake up." An almost beatific smile forms around his lips. "It feels like I sometimes felt when praying. When I feel that God loves me. Then I feel like this. It's like grace." Suddenly I see his face brim over with pain.

"What is it?" I ask, concerned.

"I'll never feel grace again! I've been condemned. It feels as if this is all a punishment. I know that I won't be saved. That's worse than death. I'll never find peace. Never!" It is the shriek of doom. No animal shrieks like that. Animals die, they don't feel doomed in all eternity. It is the sound of a soul torn to shreds. I flash on the figure 8 he pulled out of his body in dream 11. He feels that he has lost eternity. The stark contrast with the bliss in mother's arms has brought the feeling out. He looks lost.

"Can you feel like that baby again?"

"I can't," he cries. "The only thing I can feel is that I'm damned. I just feel damned!"

I can see the entire weight of fundamentalist Christianity fall like a ton of bricks on top of him. He looks shattered. The atmosphere is darker than death. This is the feeling he was trying to get away from in his wish to stop being gay. This damnation makes the prospect of dying pure hell.

"How does it feel when the boys struggle out of the whirlpool?" I ask, hoping to tap into his resilience. But Christopher doesn't answer. He is inconsolable.

Why is it that analysis always seems to make things worse?

△

Two weeks later he walks up the four steps to my office without pausing and isn't exhausted when he enters. The snow has melted and the street looks drab. When I close the door behind him and look at him from the back, I notice that his clothes fit. He's obviously bought a new outfit.

"How did you get here?" I ask, expecting to get the same answer as the previous weeks.

"I drove," he says proudly, gesturing outside. I look and see his old green convertible parked across the street.

"Can you drive?" I ask, incredulous.

"I've been driving for years," he jokes. We both laugh, relieved about his remarkable improvement.

"I want to work on the Marilyn Monroe dream. I've been trying to work on it by myself, but I don't seem to get very far." He sounds rearing to go.

"You're in a good mood," I say as I go over to my desk to excavate his scribbled version of the dream from underneath a chaotic pile of papers. "The voice you heard at first, what does it seem like to you now? Was it part of the dream?" I begin, just to enter somewhere.

"I don't really know," he answers, hesitating. "I tend to think that there was a real nurse who came in after I had pulled out the breathing tube. That must make the whole emergency room go crazy. The voice sounded frantic. But it could just as well have been part of the dream. I don't know that it matters," he concludes.

"It doesn't," I agree. "Were you scared?"

"No, not at all. I just heard it. No emotion. I could hear that the nurse was scared, but I didn't feel a thing."

"What is the room like?"

"It's a large room. The light comes from behind me. I see two windows behind me. Large windows. The room is bright behind me. I'm on this high, old-fashioned hospital bed. Behind me it is bright, but in front of me it's dark as night. The line between light and dark goes in a diagonal. Behind me is the man with the dark skin." I want him to slow down; he's racing through the image.

"Tell me more about the bed you're in," I interject.

"It's metal. Like iron. It has a white kind of mattress.

▲

Sheets. Disorderly. Narrow. Too narrow for two to lie comfortably. The man is lying behind me in spoon style." He mimics with his hands how spoons are stored in a cutlery tray. "We're close together. We haven't had intercourse. I don't know how we got there together."

"Describe the color of his skin."

"Olive. A little oily. I don't go for those guys. But we seem to be very close. We somehow belong together."

"Are you touching?"

"No, but we are very very close," he says thoughtfully.

"What are you thinking of?"

"We belong together in some way," he muses.

I make a heroic effort not to interpret and succeed, letting him stew in his sense of connection.

"He looks dead," Christopher observes.

"Is he?"

"Not really. Close, though."

"From what perspective do you see through my eyes on the behind your back?"

"I'm the one on the bed, and I see through my eyes on the bed. But I have another perspective. It's the perspective from above. From that perspective I can see the entire room. The light and the dark part. That's the position I'm describing him from. Seen from above."

"Do you feel differently in those two perspectives?"

"On the bed, all I want is to live. I want desperately to live. I'll do anything to live, anything!" His face is flustered. "I'll take the blood away from her, from Marilyn. I want to live. I want to live!" he bursts out.

I feel tears on my cheeks but don't move to wipe them away.

Silence.

"And from above?" I ask.

"I just observe. I see it all. I'm curious, at most , if anything. Not much feeling."

"Distant?"

"Not really distant either. Just there."

"Dead?"

"No, not dead. Nothing to do with death or life. Just present in the room."

"A witness," I conclude.

He nods, relieved by the naming.

"What happens when you are the Christopher on the bed and you look straight ahead?"

"I look straight at Marilyn Monroe. It is this photograph of her surrounded by a marquee. When I stare at her for a long time, the dream image itself comes back...because in the dream she was entirely three-dimensional and a picture at the same time."

"A hologram?"

"No, a real woman, just framed. That's the part of the dream I've been working on by myself. That's also where it stops. I can't get further than staring at her, and then she becomes three-dimensional. We are very closely connected. We share the same blood line. And I need the blood. She doesn't care anyway, she's already killed herself."

"Does she want to be dead?" I inquire.

"No, she doesn't want to be dead. But I want to be alive. And she has already killed herself. That's a fact." He sounds defensive. He doesn't quite feel all right about taking her blood.

"And all you can think about is that you need the blood."

"I want to live!"

"Look at her," I suggest.

His eyes remain open, but I can see his focus wander to a point behind his eyeballs.

"Is she three-dimensional?" I begin the induction of the image.

He nods, "She's looking back. We're looking at each other. We're on the same lifeline. Should I do something?" he asks me for guidance.

"No, just look at each other. Feel the lifeline."

"Nothing happens. We just keep looking at each other."

I have an expression on my face as if to begin a sentence, though I have no idea what's going to come out.

▲
_____

"Wait," he says, "wait, she wants to say something." He waves his hand in a silencing gesture. We wait. "She says: 'All I wanted was to be touched as a person and loved and appreciated.' I feel sorry for her. No, it's compassion. I touch her." He stops, looking inward in surprise.

"She's changing. She's becoming some kind of earth mother. Like in the river dream."

"Stay with Marilyn," I try, in an attempt to keep the two images from fusing.

"I can't distinguish them from each other anymore," he says. "Marilyn is now that earth mother."

If the imagination insists on fusion, it is futile to try to keep images distinctly separate.

"I want to ask her something," he says, as if he wants my permission to ask her a question. I motion him to go ahead.

"I have just asked her to tell me about the figures 8 we had pulled out of ourselves." Pause. "She says that they were vital organs. Their texture is wet and supple cartilagelike material, bendable and flexible. She also insists that it could probably be put back in by the right skilled hands—like a good physician's. I tell her that it seems impossible to me because of their size and shape."

"Does she answer?"

"She is encouraging me. She's giving me hope that it can. She's very positive."

It seems to me that her veins have already opened, feeding Christopher with her life's blood. She is the lonely Star of the Night, the Earth Mother who sacrifices herself so that her child may live. I remember the pelican in early Christian symbology, which is said to feed her own blood to her young by piercing a hole in her chest. She is likened to Christ.

At the same time I identify with the skillful physician who can put the supple vitality back into his innards. Even I notice the magical savior inflation that comes with this identification, but I can't help it. I have to be that savior-doctor. He must be kept alive! The biological survival force has taken an inexorcisable hold of me, steering me instinctively to the desire to save Christopher's life. I realize that I am too much sold on the interpretation that this vital organ he has pulled out of himself is his immune system. And that putting it back in will once again make him immune to diseases. Though I can see the psychological implications of the actual dream metaphor—saying that a vital suppleness, organic to Christopher, has to reenter his being—I can't get away from the literal heroic battle to save Christopher from the jaws of AIDS. I feel like the little Dutch boy who can stem the flood of AIDS with his finger in the dike.

△

"Last night I talked to Marilyn–Earth Mother again," he announces upon entering the room.

"How did that come about?" I ask.

"Well, I was trying to think of the dark person's name, but I couldn't get one that fit. And then I suddenly thought of asking Marilyn–Earth Mother. For some reason I was sure that she'd know. I turned to her, and she looked at me and said, with absolute certainty, 'His name is Peter.' I had to agree that, of course, his name was Peter. Now I remembered again. It was as if I had forgotten it at first and now I remembered. And I cringed at the implication."

"Why?" I ask in Dutch innocence.

At first he doesn't understand that I don't understand. He looks at me questioningly as I convey drawing a blank.

"Peter," he insists, more loudly, as if that would make me understand.

"I don't know what you're talking about," I exclaim.

"Peter, cock, dick," he says, friendly now, suddenly remembering that I am a foreigner. I nod.

"So you were cringing at the implication," I say to reconnect to the image.

"Yes." He's immediately back into it. "And then she told me that she had been caring for him. I looked at him and could see that he was doing a lot better. Peter was still very quiet. And then she said, 'What you had interpreted as his indifference isn't that at all. It's just that Peter had been *very* unconscious. But with my help,' she said, 'he is responding and coming back to life.' Then I saw him smile, and the three of us did a little dance holding hands, in a line, facing forward."

The end has me a little suspicious. It sounds too pretty. The acute survival optimism can drive us too far, cutesifying a curse.

"Can you look at him when he smiles at you before you start your little dance?"

"I'll try," he says, concentrating.

"Where do you see him?"

"He's sitting up on the bed. He's still kind of groggy, but he's got his eyes open and he's smiling at me."

"What kind of smile?"

"Kind of childlike. Naive, I'd say. I can believe her when she says that he's been very unconscious. He looks like a boy in an adult body. Very young for his age. He's not my type. But we belong together. He just sits there smiling. I can hear her words, that he's been so very unconscious. I see that she is obviously right. Her words have this ring of truth to them."

"What do you make of it, that Peter has been *very* unconscious?" I say, mimicking his intonation.

Christopher blushes again. He looks flustered. Then he bursts out: "I've always been passive in sex. I've always had men inside of me. That's what I liked and that's why I've got AIDS. If I'd been more active, I would've had a better chance of not getting it. I think Peter loved being passive, let things just happen to him. That made us sick. I'm sure that's it."

I wonder if Christopher's love for the passive role in sex also has to do with my intuition that he is identified with woman and wants to be one; with my sense that he is flustered at having a cock(s-comb) instead of a rose, combined with his inability to deploy his tool. I am reminded of the coronation of the queen and Christopher's disgust of "queens," leading to his fear of being thought effeminate. Maybe the life force has to be siphoned away from his identification with the star-struck image of woman (Marilyn) to awaken a potent sense of masculinity. But I can't bring this up without becoming overly interpretative, thereby drying up the process and probably leading directly into powerful resistances. Interpretation is an astringent agent, useful to tighten matter when it flows all over the place. But the present movement has its own inner direction.

"What is it like to have a man inside of you?" I ask instead.

"It makes me feel strong and giving at the same time," he says, blushing. "I love to give pleasure."

"You love to give," I repeat his words. "Do you also like to be inside a man?"

He nods eagerly. "But it is not as fulfilling," he adds.

"Have you made love with many men?"

He looks shy. "Very many," he says softly. I suddenly feel very attracted to him and wonder what it would be like to make love with him, even in his present skeletal shape.

"Is it easy for you to get men?" I wonder out loud.

"Not now," he mutters, sour. Then he grins. I realize that we haven't even begun to touch the issue of not being attractive anymore. We can get to that later.

"But in Florida, for instance."

"I could get anyone I wanted," he says proudly.

"How come?" I ask, realizing right away that he might take it as an insult—as if I couldn't imagine why men would be attracted to him. But he doesn't take it that way.

"Maybe because I'm well endowed," he grins, flirtatious.

"You have a big one?" I hear myself ask. We both blush, embarrassed about this intercourse, and giggle nervously.

He continues quickly, "I have a very easy contact with people. When I'm in a bar, people just come up to me and begin to tell me their life stories. People always talk to me. They seem to know that I'm a good listener."

"Is there any other reason why Marilyn–Earth Mother judges Peter unconscious, do you think?"

"She says that it has to do with what I always thought was indifference."

"In the same way that Marilyn said of herself that she was never touched or appreciated," I add, glad to feel the erotic tension between us lessen.

"Maybe I've always felt that everyone was indifferent toward me. That no one really cared."

"And maybe that fueled your sex drive," I say, no longer capable of resisting interpretation. The remark closes our conversation and makes us thoughtful.

We shake hands warmly when he leaves. I notice how sensuous the palm of his hand feels. Then I go to the back to wash my hands, like a surgeon after an operation. I think of him while washing carefully.

5

Marilyn Monroe, toward the closure of her life, in the early sixties, said, "In the end, gravity catches up with us all."

At the beginning of our next session it feels as if Christopher has been floored by gravity. His footstep on my stairs had sounded stronger, with more biological vitality, while at the same time dragging, depressed.

I see immediately that his spirit has collapsed. All my alarm bells go off. Maybe now that he is physically stronger, he is able to feel the full impact of his situation, and his situation is very depressing. But he won't be able to face it with a hollow spirit. His eyes look hollow. They don't have the defiant fire they had last week. Still, I have no intention to cheer him up. That feels banal at this point. So I wait. When the silence becomes uncomfortable, he tells me a dream from his brown corduroy dream book.

Dream 14

I remember the setting of a house that was old looking - medieval and a woman named Sarah with a black and white animal—zebralike—tied outside.

Later I was standing in the back of a crowd watching something, and I and another man accidently bumped in the crowd. He displayed intense anger like he wanted to beat me up. He was big and very attractive, but angry. I reached over and took his hand which was big and very warm and soft, imploring him that he not be so angry. Come on, we should be friends, I said, and he calmed down and even smiled a half shy, endearing smile.

"It's a dirt road. The house is on the right. It is a house with two stories and some kind of a little turret. An inn, maybe. Yes, it's an inn. And the woman is going in to get something to drink or eat. The zebra is standing outside. That's the image I remember best, that zebra. He's waiting for her. He's worn out and thirsty. Just waiting." As Christopher pronounces the word *waiting,* his shoulders slump even more than they already did.

"Can you try to feel your shoulders?" I ask.

He looks at me, not comprehending.

"What do your shoulders feel like?" I rephrase.

I see them sagging even more profoundly and know that he is feeling it. That seems to be the atmosphere of the first section of the dream as it lives inside his body. Therefore, that is the physical mood I want to reestablish upon entering the image.

"What is the road like?" I ask before he can answer my question about his shoulders. I don't want his verbal answer. He has already responded in body language.

"It's a country road. Sand. Ocher. The road leads far into the distance. There's only one house along the road. It looks like a medieval-inn kind of building. The color of the stone is similar to that of the sand. There is little contrast. Except the animal. He's black and white."

"So that stands out?"

"Yes, the animal stands out. I hardly remember the woman."

"But you know her name is Sarah?"

"Yes. But I don't know any Sarah. Maybe Abraham's wife. But I really don't know. Maybe she had a long dark dress, but I can't really remember. It's a guess. She goes inside, and the animal just has to wait. And the sun is beating down. Now I remember. The sun was beating on the animal and he just had to wait there, patiently like a mule. But he was like a zebra."

"Could you please stand up," I request gently.

Christopher looks at me, surprised. I've never asked him to get up from his chair before. He gets up with some difficulty and has a hard time getting his balance. I ache for him, feeling his weakness in my gut.

"Could you show me how the animal stands?" I ask.

Suddenly he sags so much that he almost falls over and can just barely aim for the chair behind him. Thank God he doesn't collapse onto the rug.

"What was that like?" I ask, concerned.

"Like fainting."

"Is the animal fainting?"

"Something inside the animal is fainting. Something just can't stand the wait and can't stand the heat."

"What is that something?"

"His force. He has no power to stand up anymore. It is like a fountain when the water is turned off. That's what it feels like. A fountain where the water is turned off. It just collapses into itself."

"Like a black hole," I mumble, softly enough so that he can't hear. He looks questioningly. I don't want to move out from the dream by discussing astrophysical mythology. I want to stay in, close to the image.

"I wondered what the black and white was all about," I lie.

"It seems somehow appropriate," he says, less depressed. "It's the only contrast in the landscape."

"The animal of contrasts," I suggest. "He has a white stripe and then a black stripe and a white stripe and a black stripe. For the zebra, darkness and light alternate. What is it like to be a white stripe?"

He looks puzzled.

"Just try to feel your lightest mood. When you feel that everything has meaning and serves some kind of purpose, like feeling grace."

"I can't feel that now," he groans.

"Maybe you're in the black stripe now," I conclude. "The zebra feels one phase after the other. White stripe, black stripe, white stripe, black stripe." I pause.

"Like the two sides of the hospital room," he flashes.

I nod enthusiastically. His spirits rise.

"Let's go to the man you bumped into. What is the crowd like?" I open up the next image.

"It's a crowd like at Vegas. At a boxing ring. Mainly men. Everyone is very excited. I look down on what's happening in the center. It is in some kind of sloping pit, flushed with lights. The crowd is cheering. A lot of commotion. Then I bump into him."

"What is that like?"

"At first I'm off balance. Then I'm surprised at how angry he is. He is much too furious for this little bump."

"Can you describe him?"

"He's very big. Wearing a tee shirt and jeans. Blondish."

"Your type," I interject.

"Very much my type. That's why I want to be friends with him. Otherwise I would have just turned away."

"Could he have beaten you up?"

"Easily," he says with conviction. "But I was sure that he wasn't going to. I was sure that I could soothe him."

"Can you try to feel what the man is feeling?"

"He feels terribly insulted. As if I had done him the gravest injustice."

"What does it feel like, to have been done injustice to?"

"It feels like total humiliation. Like being run into the ground. Like totally unfair. He's outraged."

"Try to feel the outrage."

"It's like having been raped. Like having been convicted for no reason whatsoever. It feels like an unjust punishment. It makes you want to kill everyone. Attack at the least provocation." He sits and feels the outrage. Tears of powerlessness run down his face. "It's not fair," he cries.

"So this is the feeling you have to become friends with," I muse after a pause. This sense of outrage and unfairness has to be felt carefully inside the chaos of massive emotion. It is a specific feeling that has to be faced and communicated with. I give him some time to stew in it.

"And then he smiles," I continue, my eye on the clock. There are ten minutes left, and I want to keep some time open for immediate practical matters.

Christopher nods. "He's shy, like me. He is very gentle. He loves to be touched."

"Like Marilyn."

"Like me."

Long pause.

"What is it like at home? Is John home a lot?"

"John is wonderful for me. He's bought a new refrigerator. And he's getting a lot of flak from his family. They're scared that he's roommates with an AIDS patient. But he's taking it. He's a wonderful friend. But he's only home at night. He works during the day. So I sit and watch the soaps."

"You wait, like the zebra."

"That's right. I'm just passing time."

"Waiting to die."

He looks shocked that I said it. "How do you mean that?"

"You think your life is over," I say, neutrally.

"Don't you?"

Now I feel the survival force surge. "You live till you die. You don't die before you die. You live. You live as if you were going to live for a long time."

"But I haven't got much more than two years. Those are the statistics. I have to take care of my funeral. I don't want others to have to pay for that. I have to think about that."

"The one doesn't exclude the other. You're going to live for a long time. You're going to live your life with a long-term perspective. And at the same time you prepare your funeral."

He looks suspicious.

"What do you want to do for the rest of your life? What do you want to achieve? Dream!" I order him.

"I'd want to be a priest," he blurts out. "I want to be of service. I want to hand out the sacraments. I want to go to the seminary."

"So apply," I say.

He laughs at what he takes to be my joke.

"I'll help you apply to a seminary here in Boston. We'll get you in. Which seminary would you like to go to?"

"Episcopalian." He grins, playing along with the joke.

"I'll have a friend of mine call the dean and check into it." I speak with the authority of the survival force.

Christopher is shaken.

"Shall I call?" I ask.

He doesn't respond.

"Shall I call?" I repeat.

"Yes," he says softly.

△

"Are you crazy?" says my friend over the telephone. "You want what?"

"I believe that Christopher has to go to the seminary. I think it's his only chance for survival."

"Do you know how much such a training costs the church? AIDS patients live two years. Do you think they'd take the risk?"

"All I ask of you is to write a letter of introduction to the dean for me if I need it. That's all."

"All right," my friend sighs, knowing me. "Please keep me informed."

△

"Of course, what I said last time is ridiculous," I concede when we discuss it at the next session. "It is absurd. But then again, your situation is absurd. You're in the middle of your life and you may be close to the end of your life at the same time." My clarity sounds cruel, but I can't soften it. "You have to feel both. And besides, I think that there may be a psychosomatic factor to the AIDS process. It sounds very coincidental to me that you got pneumocystis the week after you were fired."

"But it must have been there all along. I spoke with John about it. I must have tried not to see the symptoms. Like that cold in the fall that wouldn't leave."

"But it didn't become virulent until you were fired," I insist.

"That's true," he admits. "So what?"

"When your spirits are down in the dumps, you're less defended. After you've got AIDS, you're blown wide open. You have no biological defenses, so you need spiritual ones," I say with passion.

"I've been thinking about that myself. But I haven't given it much credence. No one is talking about AIDS in that sense. At least not anyone I know." It is March of 1985, and the debate about the psychosomatic aspects of the AIDS process has hardly yet begun. The syndrome begins with a somatic infection that permanently debilitates the immune system. The process continues when opportune diseases grab hold of the opening and create severe symptoms that can lead to death. The discussion about the psychosomatic factors in the AIDS process addresses the potential of psychological processes to affect the permanently wounded immune system.

"So you're saying I should buy my grave and live as if I still had years to go," he ponders.

"Exactly."

"Maybe I could go to Harvard Extension, the continuing education program," he says tentatively, playing with the idea. "Harvard has the most interesting psychology-of-religion program. But it's very expensive."

"There are tons of colleges here," I suggest.

"But Harvard is the most interesting in terms of religion," he says firmly.

"Then you have to go to Harvard," I agree.

"Great." He grins. "I'll spend a fortune I don't have, do a master's at Harvard for two years, then go on to the seminary for three—and I have only two years to live."

We both laugh at the absurdity.

"So that's what has to happen," I say.

"And where does the money come from?" he asks.

"Let's first try the AIDS Action Committee," I propose.

"They'll see right away that I have a very realistic plan," he jokes.

"Right," I say, "and they'll come up with one hundred

thousand dollars by tomorrow. You won't have a care in the world."

For the first time since the outbreak of the disease we have a relaxed moment, shooting the bull.

Then he grows dark and serious. "But even if I got through all that alive, I could never become a priest."

"Why not?"

"Every time I try to pray, I hear nothing. God doesn't listen to me. When I used to pray, God listened. Now He is deaf."

Back in hell. I feel the cold fire of fear make me shiver and burn my stomach.

"Have you been looking further for your Christian community?" I ask.

"There's nothing here in Boston. I can't find any place I feel at home. There isn't even anyone I can talk to about my problems of being gay and being Christian. Boston is too sedate. Maybe I should go back to Houston. I've called my friends. I'm going to visit them in the spring to see if I want to move back."

"But in the meantime you have no one to talk to about what concerns you most."

He shakes his head.

"I know someone," I say. I have a friend, Will, a black minister who is very spiritual and extremely creative. I just won't tell Christopher that he's black. He can see for himself. Will is a most gifted preacher and has dealt extensively with gay Christians. Besides, he's a wonderful man.

I give Christopher Will's phone number. "You have to talk about this with a preacher who can give you the sacraments. I can't do that." I realize that he needs the sacraments, the blood and the body of his Savior, as much as he needs the experimental AZT (the potentially life-extending AIDS drug) program he is fighting to get into, against strong medical opposition because he doesn't fit the category of test persons. (The criterion: Less than two months post-pneumocystis. Christopher was more than three months after his first attack when they finally let him in.)

Imagine, a kike sending a faggot to a nigger to save his Christian soul. The pious brethren of his childhood would have been aghast.

△

From the brown corduroy dream book.

Dream 15

Dream of putting on shoes—they were high-top work boots. At once I could feel something alive in one of them. When I pulled it off out came a big spider and a huge bumble-bee. Later I remember driving; the steering wheel was to the right.

Picture the difference between a clam on the half-shell coming out of a shoe (dream 10) or a spider and a bumble bee coming from the same place. Venus on her open moistness versus the web-spinning bloodsucker. The honey of her slender, salty clam versus the sting of the fat, hairy bee who gives no honey. The juicy, inviting young woman is the other side of the spectrum in relation to the scheming widow who catches you in her invisible web. The image is reversed. Scary side up.

At the same time the steering occurs on the opposite side.

"It looks like a mirror world," I say. "With the steering wheel on the right side and all."

He looks clumsy to the point of silliness. I laugh. "What's the matter?"

"I'm looking at the wheel on the right and I feel how all my reflexes are wrong. God, will I have to get used to that!"

"People learn to drive on the opposite side," I comfort him.

"I hate the opposite side," he hisses.

"You mean...?"

"AIDS!"

6

From the brown corduroy dream book.

Dream 16

Dream of living with my "wife" in a house. We are being imposed upon by another young couple below who are not paying the rent. I feel somehow that they could harm us, though how is vague and undefined. The girl is active in silkscreening and messy things that could damage the house. In another scene they are encouraging me to eat a vegetable or fruit that grows out back. It is a cross between a green bell pepper and an avocado. The shape is like green pepper. It is somehow hollow but it is mushy like a cooked avocado. I desire it and do eat it even though I fear they could be poisoning me. Also in the backyard is an episode with a little mouse-rat-animal. It is auburn and pink type color. I'm afraid it could bite me and I try various things for it to eat. It finally accepts a tree-or plant-bud I offer it. [Followed by a little drawing of the oblong egg shape of the bud.]

"What does your 'wife' look like?"

"I can't remember her too well. The woman who stands out is the woman downstairs. I can't remember her husband either. It's a kind of large Victorian house with a deep backyard. We live upstairs. The girl downstairs is the kind of hippie woman I can't stand. The 'creative' type." He sneers. "With her silkscreening she could poison the whole house. Her place is a mess. I always keep things neat. But she lives in a pigsty. And that is very dangerous for me. I can get infections like that"—he snaps his fingers. "And then all those horrible chemicals. I worked for a printer in Florida.

51

He used all these awful chemicals. I became real good at it. After a while I ran the shop. But I still couldn't stand the chemicals."

"What is it like to be around those chemicals?"

"You feel as if you're slowly being poisoned."

"Try to feel what it is like to slowly be poisoned."

He closes his eyes and begins to sob softly.

Gradually the acute part of his realization subsides, leaving a residue of sadness.

"What does she look like?"

"She has the same long kind of dress that the earth mother was wearing. Very long hair down her back. Dark hair."

"Where do you see her?"

"I see her in the far back of the garden at the edge of the woods. Here she is at home. She knows the woods very well. She gathers herbs there. She has something witchy about her, but she's not bad. I kind of like her when I look at her now."

"Does she know the out-of-doors?"

"She spends most of her time in the garden and in the woods. She grows her own vegetables; she has a nice garden. She especially knows the part of the garden where we are standing. That is where the garden becomes woods. She spends a lot of time here. She speaks with authority when she tells me about the green vegetable and how good it'd be for me."

"Do you trust her?"

"Now I do. But not when I met her in the dream."

"What's different?"

"I seem to know her better now. Part of my distrust was that she was so strange."

I hesitate. The woman seems to have two sides. And at the moment we can only feel her knowledgeable, benevolent side. Her other side must be connected to the parasitical (doesn't pay rent) silken screener who mixes the poisons to create images. A possible sister to the spider. But I feel pulled toward the vegetable with a survival thirst that throws caution to the wind.

"Does it sound as if she knows what she's talking about?"

"She certainly has expertise around here. She shows me the vegetable and turns it over so I can see it from all sides. It's a very vital green, shining like a bell pepper that has just been polished to a sheen. It looks very attractive. I want it."

"But you feel that it could poison you," I say to slow us down.

"Yes, I still don't know if I can fully trust her."

"Now, or in the dream?"

"Also now. She could be poisoning me. I don't know. But somehow I don't care. I want that vegetable."

"What does that feel like, this 'I don't care'?"

"Like 'What the hell, I might as well.'"

"Nothing to lose."

"Right. And she insists that it might help. She's sure of it in the same way that Marilyn is certain of her words. According to her it has some medicinal value. At this point I'd try anything."

"Do you have AIDS in the dream?"

"No, not that I know of. But when she insists on the healing value of the vegetable, I want it more. I really want it. So there must have been a sense that I needed healing. This is the clearest part of the dream. I can remember wanting it badly, forgetting about the way that she keeps her house a mess and may be poisoning us all with her chemicals, and just going for the vegetable."

"You said it was mushy like a cooked avocado?"

"Yes, it is thin, almost juicy, very easy to swallow." I see how dry his lips are. His lips have been dry a lot lately. His skin looks dry. I begin to see the rubbery wet vital organ that he pulled out of himself in a different perspective. The drying process is going on physically as well. He looks like a dried-out old plant. I understand my attraction to the moist, peppery green mush: it gives his withered vegetative system renewed vital pep. Vegetative green is the color of moist Venus, the creative imagination of the Holy Spirit, of generation and of resurrection. The inversion at the ground of being (shoe) of the moist venusian calm into the venereal spider who sucks out all vital moisture may be healed with a juicy regenerative remedy that is possibly poisonous.

"Can you try and swallow it right now?"

"I can't taste it. But I can feel the substance. It slides easily down my throat. It feels as if it quenches my thirst somewhat." He licks his lips. "It somehow feels very nutritious."

"Well, you need to gain some weight anyway, so maybe you should regularly imagine eating this mush, deep in your back. It might do you good," I comment, hearing my own allusion to bone marrow.

He laughs. "Sure, why not. I'm trying to gain weight. A friend of mine who's in body building has given me a diet that should get me back to a reasonable weight pretty soon."

"Maybe you should also try tea of the echinacea root. It's an old-fashioned European remedy to boost the immune system. I'll get you a bottle of the extract." He looks at me with sarcasm in his eyes. I'm identified with the herbal hippie. I should move on quickly, but make a mental note to bring in the concentrate of echinacea root anyway. Who knows.

"What about that little rat in the last part?" I change the subject.

"I was scared shitless. If a rat bit me in the condition I'm in now I'd get a horrible infection."

"So at that point you have AIDS."

He nods. "And I'm trying all kinds of things to get rid of him. But I was very scared. I'm silent and wait. The fear time. Injuries are an entirely different ballgame now." I see the fear of death in his eyes. I'm silent and wait. The fear builds up. My intestines twist; I feel like bending over double. Then it peaks and diminishes. We look at each other, knowing that we've both felt it.

The rat demanding to be placated reminds me of the little weasel man (dream 2) whose high demands might leave one too depleted for a next crossing. The rodent nips the bud, eats the germ before it can sprout. It is striking that he emerges right after the administering of the nutritious remedy.

"What was the bud like that he finally accepted?"

"Small. Kind of oval with one end wider than the other."
He draws the oblong egg shape in the air. "Hard, very
different from the vegetable. A husk around it. Brownish."

"I'm struck by how close the healing plant and the poisonous devouring rat are."

"They do follow each other directly," he agrees. "What do
you mean?"

"Just that the benevolent and malevolent forces follow
each other closely. What that means I don't know."

"You're very helpful."

"Thank you," I say, taking a preposterous little bow from
my chair.

△

From the brown corduroy dream book.

Dream 17

*Dream of meeting young man—we had agreed to
meet, though I know not when and how we meet. I
called his hotel room and verified that he was
coming. Next thing I turn around and he is in the
room waiting for me. Someone, Ethel, had let him in.
He's very young and attractive. We kiss awhile. At
first I straighten the room. It was kind of messy.
Then in some building, I think in basement. I have to
start a mower-like machine on jointed frame. I start
it and a room of glass fills to about three feet of
water—salty or milky-looking and warm. The
machine after starting has to be unplugged and I'm
afraid it will shock me but I do it and it doesn't. We
love each other in the warm wet atmosphere but Ava
is there and can see and looks hurt. Afterwards he
goes somewhere a minute and I suggest he'd be a
good boyfriend to a young girl I know.*

"What I thought most strange about the whole dream was
the end. Why would I tell this gorgeous young man that I

have a girlfriend for him?"

I shrug my shoulders and grin in masculine conspiracy. "No idea why you would do a thing like that. A beautiful young man..."

"Exactly. That's just it!"

"Could it be related to the fact that Ava was looking on?" I wonder out loud.

"Probably," he muses. "When she looks at me, I'm reminded of how she looked when I told her we couldn't be engaged anymore. There was heartbreak in it. It hurt her terribly." His face becomes drawn and even more pale than usual. He bites the pointed nails on his long, elegant fingers. "I felt very guilty. It was awful. The choice I had to make felt awful. I can feel it again when I see her behind the glass."

"Can you describe the whole scene?"

"I'm inside this kind of aquarium. All glass. There are no metal dividers in the corners. The walls are of glass. Ava is on the outside. She has her hands on the glass. Palms outstretched. Her head in between. She is so sad! Not judgmental—hurt. It would have been so much easier if she'd been angry. But she was just looking without changing her expression. I looked back."

Silence.

"What was your contact like?" I ask.

"Somehow we both knew who we were to each other."

I maintain a question-filled silence.

"We loved each other, and we were separated by thick glass, in two different worlds. I think that the young man was my gift to her. Not to her personally but to someone like her. A girlfriend. Like having a fresh start. It was a young girl I knew, but I don't know who. She's about twelve, fourteen. Very impressionable."

"But it's with the young man in the basement that you turn on. With him the juices begin to flow. Sap rises."

"Yes, that is the clearest part of the whole dream. First I have to get the machine started." Like the contraption he can't get to work in dream 10.

"It takes a few times because I have to jump-start it. It takes a lot of effort. And I'm very surprised that it works. As soon as it begins to work, we're in this aquarium. We are both naked. He has a very strong body. No hair on his body. As the water begins to rise, we embrace each other. I kiss him. We get very turned on. The water is just to our hips, about three feet. It's kind of salty."

"Does it taste or smell like sperm?"

"Not really. It isn't as thick, and it's much more salty."

"Like clam juice?"

"That's it!"

"So he gets your venusian love juices going," I say, thinking that it makes sense as a homeopathic remedy for a venereal disease. Love's juice to treat love's disease.

"I love making love with him, if that's what you mean."

"I mean that when you're with him, the libido rises. The life juice. That's important because the moist vital organ has been pulled out. Otherwise you might dry up."

"Do you mean I have to go and find a lover?" he inquires, sarcastic.

"Isn't literal lovemaking out of the question?"

"I can masturbate with someone," he says, tense. I suddenly get scared that he might infect others.

"But you can't make love or anything dangerous," I insist.

"They explained that to me at the hospital," he notes dryly. We gaze at each other for a moment. I feel a spear of distrust pierce my side. There is a crucial issue here. We are at a standoff.

"No, I don't mean you should find yourself someone to make love with. Someone to love, yes. I think that your love of the man gives you vitality. Just think of Peter, he's hardly alive!"

"You mean a part of myself. I have to love my masculinity."

I cringe. I despise the move from this specific love for this specific man into a love of "masculinity," a cold, empty abstraction. On the other hand, it is a dim realization of the fact that all these beings populate his psychocosm, his world of interiority. It signals a move away from the fixation on literal sexual action, toward juicy sexual imaginings that feel interior and intimate. It creates the warm fluidity *in vitro,* inside the glass, so that a mixture of love juices can take place under observable laboratory conditions. I wonder if the analysis is the laboratory, and I wonder what that means to transference. The onlooker provokes guilt about his homo-eros. So as analyst-onlooker I might make him feel ashamed about the central choice in his love life. At the same time the juices are definitely already flowing between him and me.

"Yes," I say, "and love your sexual imagination. What is the young man like? Is he like Laurence?"

"No, he's more like one of the models I had when I was living the fast life in Florida. One of these anonymous guys who turn me on."

"Up to your hips," I conclude, feeling the force of the impersonal sexual imagination. This is lust—instinctive, unconcerned with relationship and with a vital validity of its own.

7

From the brown corduroy dream book.

Dream 18

Most of the people in this dream I think are young people I have known. There is at first a young beautiful man I'm attracted to and who is very friendly to me. Later in the dream he is seduced into going to bed with _____. I am jealous and am leaving but decide to watch if I can. I go around to side of house where I can see. Martha looks out and sees me. I fiddle with the screen like I'm fixing it and she thinks nothing of it.

Am going to leave again but decide to take another look. Have to walk around where dog is tied and am concerned about health and feces stipulation.

They are making the bed quickly and as I'm leaving I look up in another window and see Brendon and he sees me. I go in and glad to see each other. He has a strange punkish haircut and black and red ring.

Lady in room is opening store of such jewelry. I offer possibility of working for her if I came back to Houston, but she isn't thrilled with the idea.

"First we are together in a partylike atmosphere. A lot of my old friends and me. All my age. Good mood. Then we are in a clothing store. I see this very attractive man. There are many people milling about. I don't know them. They're around my age. I come closer to this beautiful young man. He smiles at me, and I'm very attracted to him. He is buying pants. The salesman is also very interested in him. I can see them exchange glances. The salesman must know that I'm after this man but he doesn't care. I see his hands linger longer than necessary on the hips of the man who tries the pants. I get a pang of jealousy, especially when I notice that the young man gets turned on. I find it a rotten trick of the salesman.

"Then we're in this white stucco house. It's kind of run-down, but not very. I know that the young man and the salesman are making love in one of the rooms of the house. I feel terrible and curious at the same time. Very ambivalent. Shall I leave or not? I don't know. Then I decide to peep. I get excited at the prospect. Some kind of exquisite torture. I can hear them going on. I listen at the door. Then I go out and walk around the house to find the window. They're on the ground floor.

"By the side of the house are no windows. It is like an apartment house. From above I suddenly see Martha looking at me. Martha is an older friend of mine who helped me through school a long time ago. I know that she has seen me, and I'm flustered. I must find some reason for what I'm doing here in the rain. I look around the flowers in the back of the house and notice a screen door. There's a tear at the bottom. I go over to it and pretend to fix it. I look up and see that she doesn't care what I'm doing. She just looks at me.

"The screen door is green and has two screen panels, one in the upper half, the other in the lower. The tear is in the bottom lower right. I can see into the hall of the house. I have to go over to the left a little farther in the back, through the flowerbeds, and then I can see them. Now I have to be quick or it will all be over. I look again to see if Martha is still watching. She is gone. I stop fiddling with the door and want to leave. They must be finished by now anyway. But I decide against leaving and go toward the window. I have to get past the dog. It isn't a particularly nasty dog. But it is a watchdog and he's tied to the house. I have to pass him to get to the window. I realize that with AIDS the bite of a dog or even touching him and getting his shit on me could be fatal.

"I go anyway. The dog is somehow not a problem. I get to

the window. When I stand on my toes and stretch real hard, I can just peek in. They are making the bed and I'm disappointed. They're very quick and furtive in their movements, as if they want to get out of there as soon as possible without anyone seeing them or knowing what they have done. I back out of the flowerbeds and look up to see if Martha is there again. But instead, in another window, I see Brendan. We look at each other and I'm overjoyed. I run inside through the back door and we're very glad to see each other.

"At first when I hug him he's like the Brendan I remember. Then suddenly he has this wild punk haircut and he's smaller, about twelve years old. He looks real weird. I specially notice his ring. It is black and red or blackish red. A large oval that covers half his ring finger. I ask him where he got the ring. He points up to the mezzanine. There I see a familiar-looking woman who has just opened a store to sell such rings and stuff. She looks like Maggie in Houston, but she isn't. She isn't particularly friendly. I'd love to work in her store. I like the jewelry she is selling. Especially Brendan's ring. I could imagine moving back to Houston for it. She doesn't give me the time of day. It is clear that she isn't interested in having me come back to Houston. I feel snubbed."

While he's giving the elaborate description of the dream, I notice myself fiddling with my ring a lot. I do this often. But by the end of his narrative, it takes on a specific significance. The ring on my left ring finger is a large oval, very dark red—sometimes looking almost blackish—covering almost half of my finger.

"Was the ring like mine?" I ask, pointing at my finger.

Christopher looks at it for a moment, then says emphatically: "Not at all. It doesn't look like your ring at all."

I'm surprised, because his description matched my ring so exactly. I try again. "It sounded like mine," I mumble.

"No, it wasn't!" he exclaims, annoyed.

"All right, all right, so it wasn't," I soothe him. I can only explain his annoyance as some form of resistance. It is imperative that no connections be made between Brendan, a former lover, and me. Such a connection must be very threatening. So I drop it.

"The clothing store reminds me of a store in Florida," he says pensively after a short silence.

"You used to work there?"

"No," he answers hesitatingly, almost embarrassed. There must be something about this store that is important.

"What are you thinking about?"

"We used to go to that store and steal sweaters," he says, blushing. "I would shoplift them and give them away. At some point I had a closet full of sweaters and shirts. I didn't wear them. I just had them in my closets."

"Why?"

"I don't know," he mutters, embarrassed.

I wait and let him stew for a while in his embarrassment to see what he'd come up with.

"I wanted to have them. Just have them. Have beautiful clothes. Not particularly to wear them. Just to have them in my closet and look at them every once in a while. That was the time that I worked in the print shop. I hated the ugliness of the shop. Maybe that's why I did it. To forget the day to day. I was dressed to kill." He looks down at his clothes. He's wearing a crimson sweater, designer jeans with a silver-and-turquoise-buckled Native American belt, and beautiful, well-worn cowboy boots. "I love beautiful things." He sighs.

"Like jewelry," I remark, looking at his simple golden ring with cut-out crosses. He follows my gaze.

"Friends at the seminary gave me this one. I wear it all the time." I'm conscious again of the central place of Christianity in his life. He wears his cross ring like a wedding band.

"How did you feel about shoplifting?"

"It didn't faze me at the time. I only went to large stores that didn't even notice anything missing from their inventory. I also knew exactly what to take so that they wouldn't notice it. It was kind of like a sport."

I can't help thinking of the irony of his being unjustly fired from the elegant clothing store where he worked. It also makes me wonder whether something fishy actually did happen there. I want to ask him, but I don't know how. "Did you ever do it since Florida—shoplifting, that is?" I ask him finally.

"No, it just stopped being attractive. In Florida it was some kind of compulsion. It somehow went with the fast life." He sounds sincere.

"The life of external beauty and cosmetics?"

He nods. "Superficial and wonderful. The guy in the dream is like the men I had in Florida. One of my lovers there was a model from the blue jeans ads. He was gorgeous. I was proud just to be seen with him. I was very popular. I loved it."

"So why did you leave it?"

"It got to be empty and repetitive. I wanted something more stable. It was as if I'd been running around constantly. And when I broke up with Laurence, I was afraid I'd get back into it."

"What was the salesman like in the dream?"

"He was a sleaze. Attractive and all, but he didn't think anything of taking the guy I was after. You don't do that when you're in sales. You respect the customer. And I was the customer," he concludes with tongue-in-cheek professional pride.

"What is it like to be such a sleaze?" I continue, smiling.

"At this moment I'd rather be him than me. He gets the guy, and I've got AIDS. It is exciting to be him. You get what you want. You just take what you please. You just hold out your hand and you've got it. I used to be lucky like that. Men were all over me."

I can still feel his nostalgia and my attraction to him. I'm sold. His charm still sells. His salesman charms the pants off my customer. Our silence becomes uncomfortable.

"Do you notice that this dream is similar to the one where Ava looks from behind glass at the men making love? Just that now you've changed places with Ava. But the image is similar."

He looks startled. "I hadn't thought of that. What does that mean?"

"What does it feel like to be excluded?" I ask, bypassing his question in an attempt to avoid speculation.

"I feel very jealous."

"Stand by the window again," I suggest.

He closes his eyes.

"Where are you standing?"

"I'm looking in already. I see them quickly making the bed. I can hardly stretch myself tall enough to see them. The room looks beige. It's like a motel room. They're dressed, and silent; they're not talking to each other. It looks as if they feel guilty. No, I feel guilty. That's why I look up again to see if Martha is still there. I still like that man who bought the pants." He is quiet for a moment, apparently feeling the sexual attraction. I wait.

"Now I'm standing fixing the screen door. I can hear them behind me. They're making enough noise for me to hear. I have tears of envy. I want to be in there making love. Instead I'm screwing around with a screen."

"Screened out," I interject. He looks puzzled. I don't explain. I just wanted the words *screen* and *shut out* to reverberate with each other. The term *screen memory* pops up, which Freud used to describe a memory that stands in for one that is too painful to remember. But I don't know what to do with it, so I ask instead, "Are you standing while you screw around with the screen?"

"No, I kneel down on one knee. I work feverishly. I want Martha to think I'm really doing something. But it's strange; somehow I'm inside the house and I see Martha stand next to me. She's wearing a house dress and an apron. She just looks at me."

"What kind of look is it?"

"I don't want her to know what I'm here for. I don't want her to know. I don't want her to know!" Suddenly he has heard his words with a different meaning. "I don't want her to know I have AIDS. She took care of me. She helped me through college before I went to the seminary. I don't want to see her when I go to Kansas next May. And I don't want to tell Hank when I go see him in Kentucky in May. He's been in an old-age home since Ethel died. I don't want to go and tell him that I will probably be dead before him. I can't tell him that!" He looks sorrowful. "Kentucky is beautiful in May," he muses.

"Why does Martha's look make you feel guilty?"

"It's so steady, so knowing. I don't want her to know that I'm following these men around."

"Does she know you're gay?"

"No. She helped me when I'd just gone off to college and had no money to finish my studies. She is a very pious Christian woman. She helped me because she said that I'd be able to help others someday." Christopher chokes up. "What a waste!" he whispers. His eyes stare into a deep, dark hole in space.

"Did Hank and Ethel know you were gay?"

"No. It didn't make sense to tell them. I just said when I left the seminary that I'd changed my mind. It would only have hurt them. They could never have understood. To them faggots were the worst kind of abomination before the Lord."

"To you too?"

"I probably hate faggots just as much as they do." He's disgusted with himself.

"In the last dream it was Ethel who let your young lover in, though. Remember?"

"I could never figure that one out. What do you make of that?"

"Maybe she wants your juices to flow again, seduce you back to life. Maybe the young man is her envoy. Maybe Ethel opens the door to the fountain of youth." Christopher looks old and bent as if every drop of youth has been drained from him. Ethel might have control over the sap of life, the bio-force that makes sprouts grow. Sprouts way back in the garden where the pink rat lives who eats them (dream 16). Epitome of feminine paradox! "Has Ethel ever been seductive with you?" I ask.

"No. she always wore an old house dress. She looked a bit slovenly, never got dressed up. She cared for me; she took me to church. I was fond of her but not in the least bit attracted." It sounds true.

"Was your real mother attractive?"

"I don't know. I never saw her," he replies curtly. Clearly he doesn't want to talk about his natural mother. He must hate her and be terribly hurt by her, but he doesn't want to think about it. The resistances are massive, and I feel that we won't get closer to his feelings about his birth mother. He looks away; there's something stubborn about him.

"What's Brendan like?" I ask after a silence that's lasted too long.

"At first he is himself," Christopher says, glad to get out of the impasse. "But then he becomes this odd, wild-looking kid. I don't like punk. It's a style I find very unattractive. I like his ring, though."

"What is it like to be such a punk?"

"He's very rebellious. He doesn't take no for an answer. He's also vulnerable. Very vulnerable. When I look at him in that way, I feel protective of him."

"What does it feel like, that vulnerability and the protectiveness?"

He sits quietly for a moment, feeling both feelings simultaneously. "Like a mother and a baby," he says softly. I'm reminded of dream 12, where Christopher ends up in the arms of the mother by the river. I give him some time to let the feeling sink in. Then I look at the clock. The hour is almost over, and I still want to know about the jewels and the jeweler. Especially since she makes rings like mine. Her jewels might shed light on the relationship between Christopher and me.

"Tell me about the jewelry store on the mezzanine." I seem to wake him from a creamy reverie. At first he doesn't know what I want him to do. I urge him to describe the store to me again.

"It's light. A lot of glass. Glass display boxes. Beautiful jewelry. Big stones. Indian belt buckles. I like belt buckles." I again notice his silver Native American belt buckle with the large turquoise on it. It goes well with his high-heeled, beautifully worked leather boots.

"Any jewelry in particular that you remember?"

"No. But nothing is as exciting as Brendan's ring."

"Tell me about the jeweler."

"She's like Maggie, my friend in Houston."

"The one from your Christian community who said you could come back to Houston any time and live with her?"

"Yes, but the jeweler is a very different character than Maggie. She doesn't want me to come back to Houston at all. Maggie is more like Martha. They've both been very helpful in time of need. Both good Christian women."

"What is this woman like?" I ask, referring to the jeweler.

"She doesn't give me the time of day. She's much too busy. She has no time for me at all."

"Concentrate on her."

"She's very busy. She is constantly rearranging things. Moving something an inch over to this side, picking something up, putting it down in the same place. She looks restless. She's got a shawl over her head. She's blond, hair up. I ask her if I can work for her. She stands with her back to me. We're apparently in Houston, 'cause I tell her I'd move back there. She turns around."

"What kind of expression does she have on her face?"

"She doesn't want to take care of me. She doesn't want to be responsible for me. She doesn't really want me at all. I'm just taking up her time. Can't I see that she is busy? That's all written in her face." Christopher looks dejected. "I feel unwanted," he says listlessly.

Behind his sallow old sharp-featured face I see the unwanted round-faced baby. Maggie the Jeweler is the embodiment of maternal duplicity: the Maggie who lives in Houston is a promise of shelter and love, while the jeweler figure abandons him. Like his grandmother and his mother.

8

"I met with Will," he says. It is a typical New England afternoon in early April—so cold and dank that it might just as well have been February. He is coughing some, and we're both apprehensive about his developing a cold. We look at each other knowingly when he spits into a tissue. "Don't worry," he declares as he tosses the tissue into my wastepaper basket. "You won't get AIDS from my phlegm." I know this and nod. We exchange melancholy smiles.

"How did you like Will?"

"I liked him." Pause. "Did you know he was black?" Christopher asks in a noncommittal tone.

"Of course," I exclaim, feigning not to understand his question. "Will's a friend of mine. He's a great preacher. He's creative, a devoted Christian, and he's a wonderful human being. That's why I sent you to him. Does it matter to you that he's black?" I add innocently.

"No," Christopher answers with only the slightest hesitation. "It sure took me by surprise, though."

"Why?"

"I told you how they thought about blacks where I grew up."

"You mean niggers?"

"Right."

"Like faggots."

"Right."

"Tell me about niggers. Just list everything you can think about from your childhood as far as blacks are concerned. Give me a list of adjectives."

Christopher is silent. He looks embarrassed.

"I know it's not what you think now anymore. But I just

want to know more about your background."

"Well," he begins haltingly, "Blacks are—"

"Niggers," I interrupt. I don't want disinfected rationality. I want to hear the reverberation of the racism in his background.

He smiles shyly. "They're lazy." He hesitates again, clearly abashed. I nod in encouragement. "They don't want to work," he adds. I nod again. "They're dumb, thick-skulled." He's starting to speak more rapidly as his background begins to speak autonomously. "They're dirty, stinky, and sweaty. They're gullible and passive." Then he catches himself. "But that's not what I think now!"

"I know. Now you know differently. You're thirty-seven years old."

"But there were other things too. They're vulnerable; they've been abused and enslaved. They're supposed to be unconscious. They live and worship in collectives. And they have deep feelings and beautiful children. They love their children. I love black children. I think they're beautiful."

"Who says all that stuff about their being dumb and dirty and all those kind of things?"

He looks at me, noncomprehending.

"Who in your background speaks that way about blacks?"

"Everyone did. All the pious Christians," he replies with disgust. "All the devout fundamentalists who lived by the Bible. We were all racists. That was the norm." He looks sick to his stomach about his upbringing.

"Tell me more about your fundamentalist brethren," I request, curious about something I had only read about in books.

"We're helpers and healers of others," he begins, his voice dripping with sarcasm. "We just need one sickie and we're in business. We get our authority straight from the Lord; we abide by the law and we condemn anyone who transgresses it. We're ready to judge, always prepared to tell it like it is, to preach to everyone whether they want to listen or not. We exude superiority and condescension, and we're basically uninvolved with other people's misery. We give them loads of good advice but don't make any effort to really help. We're inflexible and inflated." His voice has become ever more bitter throughout this litany. "We love preaching to others because we know how things are, we know the truth," he adds.

"You wanted to be a preacher," I say softly. "A fundamentalist preacher."

"I still want to be a preacher," he answers quietly. "But not like that. Not to tell people how to live their lives. I want to be a preacher to be with people in their pain and help them to ask questions, help them to find God. Help myself to find God."

I ask him to write down the whole litany in his dream book so that he doesn't forget what his Christian shadow-world looks like. These are Christians of the ilk of the dream jeweler who rejects Christopher in his time of need. This is the shadow play of the imagination where all the shades we keep locked away from ourselves come to life. Shades from the distant past, like the ones who kicked him out of the seminary for being a faggot.

"So you like Will?"

Christopher nods emphatically. "He has thought a lot about the question of gays in the church. We've been talking about that. And about confession and absolution. Last Sunday I was in his church. I received the host, I passed the peace, and I felt communion. I haven't felt that for a long time."

Thank God for Will.

△

From the brown corduroy dreambook.

Dream 19

Dream of Ethel running out of back of house down to a pier acting as if she wanted to jump in and end her life. The way she looked back the second time to see if I was watching gave it away that she just wanted attention.

"It's a white house with land sloping down to the water. There's a large wooden pier on stilts. It's high above the water. I'm standing on the left of the house, and I see her rush out the back door down to the dock. She looks desperate. I see her look all around as she is running. I know she's looking to see if I am around to notice her. She runs down the meadow and across to the pier. I see her look around again. Now I know she is aware of my presence and wants to cast me a last desperate look before killing herself. I realize that it's all an act for my benefit. She's desperate and just wants attention."

"Do you ever feel like killing yourself?" I ask.

"Yes, but not really."

"What do you mean?"

"I mean that whenever I begin to seriously think about it, I know I can't do that before God. It feels wrong. I want to live," he says.

"What does it feel like when you seriously feel like it?" I ask obstrusely but with perfect clarity.

"I want to do it. I really do. I want to be out of all this. Just gone. But then I come up against the certainty that I can't kill myself."

"Not out of cowardice but out of the implicit impossibility," I infer.

"Exactly," he replies.

Pause.

"Did Ethel ever behave like that?"

"No, she was very level-headed. No, this isn't like her at all. She wasn't dramatic like that."

"How is she different from Ethel in the dream?"

"Ethel in the dream looks like an actress giving a performance."

"So she isn't really desperate?" I inquire.

"No, I mean she doesn't really intend to kill herself."

"But she is really desperate."

"Yes, she is," Christopher agrees.

"What does her despair feel like?"

▲

"It's like a black raging ocean," he answers, not feeling it.
"I've often thought about what it feels like and sometimes I
feel it. I felt it when I was standing on the second-floor
landing wanting to throw myself down the stairs because it
had almost killed me to get up there."

Like Ethel.

"What does it feel like?" I ask again.

"I can't feel it right now. I sometimes feel it when I'm
home alone. I often feel like it then. It's like screaming and no
one hearing you. It feels empty."

Pause.

"Is Ethel desperate because of you? You're her son."

"I don't know," he replies, honest.

"Try to feel her despair. Hers, not yours."

"I can't." He looks sorry about not being able to please me.
He wants to feel despair for me, but he can't deliver. I feel
demanding. I would want him to feel what it is like for the
fishwoman to see her fishchild (dream 5) waste away with
AIDS. Mother might be drowning in despair already, and she
might not really want to drown herself literally. But since he
can't feel it, it makes no sense to me to pursue the relation
between Ethel and the Fishwoman any further. We would
end up in speculation. The despair of a mother losing her
child stays with me. What do you feel, Mother of the Son?

△

From the brown corduroy dream book.

Dream 20

Dream of being at Nan's house for dinner or party.
The animals are being very unruly and for some
reason I'm the only one who seems to be bothering. I
am being very domineering with them and at one
point a cat scratches me in a sore on my wrist. Very
dangerous for me.

"Nan keeps a very clean house. Whenever I go to Nan
everything is always spotless. I like it that way. I like a very

clean and neat home."

"Like when you were the landlord in the dream of the hippie woman and the avocado. The printmaker was making a mess in your house, and you hated it."

He nods in acknowledgment. "I'm sitting on the couch, and the animals are all over. They are very untrained and unruly. They're all over me. I get upset—with the animals and with Nan, who doesn't seem to care. I believe there are others in the room, but I can't remember. I use my most authoritative tone of voice. At some point I yell at them. But they get ever more unruly." I'm reminded of the rat in the back of the avocado garden. "Now I get scared. I have sores on my wrist. The cat scratches me. I realize that I have AIDS and that I'm in grave danger."

"At the end in the avocado dream there was a pink rat who threatened to bite you."

"Yes, but here I actually got bitten. I don't like dogs or cats."

"But you used to have two Afghans!" I interject.

"Those are different. They're not really dogs. They're more like works of art. Special creatures in a category all by themselves. These are mutts and alley cats. Ordinary cats and dogs."

"Closer to rats?"

"Yes."

"What do you feel like when you realize that you've been bitten?" It seems to me that since now he's actually been infected by the animal, he's ready to feel it. It might have reached his self-awareness.

"At first I'm furious. I want to kill the cat. But that's over pretty soon. Then I feel like falling down a hole in the ground and I'm scared to death. That's when I wake up."

"What's the fury like?"

"I could strangle that cat. Tear him to shreds. Make him hurt like hell. I'm ready to kill." His jaws are grinding like a rabid dog's. I'm reminded of the man who got furious when Christopher bumped into him in the back of the crowd of spectators.

"You look furious," I conclude.

He grins. My remark had sounded very dry.

I can feel the fear at this moment, not so much the fury.
"What's the fear like?" I ask.

"I can't feel it now," he begins.

I wait. "What is it like to have sores on your hands?" I ask
after a while.

"Sometimes I'm scared shitless that I'll get deformed," he
acknowledges.

"Kaposi's sarcoma?" I wonder, referring to the dread
disease that AIDS patients are prone to, deforming their
bodies with tumors and sores.

"I don't want to become disgusting," he utters, revolted.

I can feel his love of beautiful surfaces twist anxiously in
my stomach. It gives access to our dread.

"What would it be like to get Kaposi's?" I press.

"I couldn't look at myself anymore. I'd rather die."

"Really?"

"No, but almost. I'd really feel like an appalling leper. I'd
feel excommunicated. Deserted. Isolated." He shivers.

"You feel isolated," I echo his words.

I can feel dread grip him, tearing him downward, away
from me.

He's gone.

I feel deserted and lonely.

△

From the brown corduroy dream book.

Dream 21

Dreamed I got herpes.

"At first I was elated. Herpes! I felt ridiculous. It didn't
matter at all. I'd *love* to have had herpes. Wouldn't bother me
at all! Then I realized that with AIDS, herpes could kill me,
and I got scared again."

Like with the scratch of the cat.

"But what stayed with me most was the irony of it. How relative things are. How insignificant herpes was!"

△

I've been asked to speak at the grand rounds at Mount Auburn Hospital of Harvard Medical School. I want to give a first report on Christopher's dreams, up to the Marilyn dream. He is very pleased.

"Feel free to use any material of mine," he insists. It gives him satisfaction that his material can be useful to others. During the coming months he explicitly reiterates this point, adding that his dreams are all he has to give.

The tenor of my lecture at the hospital is that Christopher is an individual, not a statistic. I'm upbeat and don't understand the certainty of the entire medical staff present that Christopher will surely die. I get angry with medical doctors. My anger at AIDS gets transferred to them.

"How did it go?" he asks eagerly during the session after the lecture.

"They don't understand the psychosomatic underpinnings of AIDS," I say, irritated. "They don't see that you came down with symptoms when you got fired, so that there must be a psychosomatic component. As long as we can keep your spirit strong, we're in good shape. You now have to forge spiritual antibodies! A psychological immune system!" I exclaim.

He doesn't answer. I can see his doubts. *We can lick this,* the John Wayne-like survival force whispers in my ear.

△

We never had a chance to work on the following dream, another orphan from the brown corduroy dream book:

Dream 22

Dream of riding this huge elephant with Ava. She is dressed elegantly and later the elephant is replaced by a wonderfully beautiful antique open carriage.

I see the images of *Around the World in Eighty Days,* a

movie from my childhood with suave David Niven and princess Shirley MacLaine. I see them sway on the waving backs of oceanic elephants, languid and elegant, breezing through the air; Ava, his erstwhile fiancée, and Christopher, driver of elephants. They are on top of the world. I feel high, elated, wind in my hair. I see a genteel world of beauty from before the time that life turned to rot. This nostalgia about a golden age of riding high in the open carriage of days long past contrasts sharply with the images from the next dream in the brown corduroy dream book.

Dream 23

Friends show up in my convertible but without the dogs. I am uncomfortable with that and go to get them. They are Afghans and valuable and I have lost one before. Get to where they are and call and they come and jump in the car but a huge dog of another breed (like a Dane) gets in too. He is so huge I make him get out. I pick up the people and driving along notice the gas must be about to run out any second. Someone has driven it all out and not replaced it or told me. The car runs out of gas and stops, fortunately in front of a construction sight [sic] where I think I can buy a little gas cause I see a couple of cars. I awake. At another point I kept relating in the dream as one of the conscripts and remember struggling for that word as though the word itself were important. At another point am eating at a cafeteria-like place, apparently in my shoes and undies. Ava comes in as I am going to get something. I tell her where to sit and feel embarrassed at being unclothed.

"I'm in Florida on a boulevard next to a beach. I hear someone honk the horn behind me and I turn around. I see my car. I've lent it to my friends. I don't remember who they are. Some generic Florida friends. Very carefree. Not caring at all about the fact that they've left my dogs somewhere—

they don't even know where. They laugh. I get worried. I lost one dog once. I'm sure it was stolen. Precious dogs often get stolen in Florida. I'm annoyed with them, with their careless attitude. I get in the car and tell the others I'll be right back. They leave. I think they stroll toward the beach.

"I tear away, looking for the dogs. I find them at a large parking lot. No cars. The dogs are playing, running after each other. I come up to the fence, stop the car, and call to them. I'm in my green convertible. The roof is down. The sun is out, and the dogs are having fun. When they hear me, they turn around, see me, and run right to the car, and jump in. But they're followed by this huge dog I've never seen before. He takes up the whole back seat. He's happy; tongue out of his mouth, panting. I'm annoyed. With that dog in the car, no one else will fit. He just takes up too much space. The dogs are waiting for me to start my car. But I want the Great Dane out. I turn around, get up on my knees in the driver's seat and start pulling the Dane over. He is very heavy and hardly moves. With some effort I'm able to shove him out.

"Somewhere along the boulevard I pick up these same people from the beginning who had borrowed my car. The drive I don't remember very well. Just that it's long and has some episodes to it: the one of looking for the word *conscript* and the other scene in the cafeteria with Ava in my underwear. I just remember the embarrassment and feeling exposed. I have a clear memory again at the point where I'm driving by myself and I see the fuel gauge practically on zero. I'm angry. I'm upset with these people who used up all the gas without telling me or filling it back up. I can't stand it how thoughtless they are. Totally self-absorbed! At that moment the car runs out of gas. At a construction site. By the way, I spelled it s-i-g-h-t in my dream book."

"As if they're working on your sight, your vision?"

"'Maybe. In any case, I see them building this house. The walls are up. Gray concrete, two stories. Cars parked next to a pile of sand and rubble. I hope they'll let me siphon off some of their fuel. As I wake up, I'm aggravated and relieved at the same time."

I am reminded of Christopher's frequent assertion that he gets life from the living.

△

"That was a huge dog, wasn't it?" I try, jumping into the dream at a point that attracts me. Long dreams ask for a leap of faith down from the rostrum of utter bafflement.

"Enormous. I've never seen a dog that big."

"Is he a friend of your Afghans?"

"They were playing together."

"How is he different from your dogs?"

"He's not beautiful. Just big. Not graceful. Just large and lumbering. My dogs have lovely auburn hair. I used to love to see their long hair wave in the wind as I drove with them. Everyone would turn around and look at us."

Like beautiful women, I think to myself, seeing the three of them cruise along the beach in the green convertible. "Why do you kick the Dane out of the back seat?" I inquire.

"He's just too big. I can't handle his size."

"You can't handle his size in back," I joke mischievously, at the same time pondering what it would be like to be the big animal in his back.

Christopher grins in complicity. "I've never had that problem," he replies. The atmosphere gets heated. The unspoken taboo on discussing our undercurrent sexual relationship makes us uncomfortable.

"The dog would mess up the car. He's too big to take with me. He'd break things. And besides, I don't want to take care of a Great Dane. Too much responsibility. And he isn't my dog," Christopher speaks quickly, taking the edge off the ambiguous sexualized atmosphere.

Compared with the previous dream, the huge animal is here inside the carriage instead of being ridden. The huge animal power which in olden days carried him now has become an overburdening load on his back. Driving on empty; vitality used up till the last drop.

"Who were those people who lost your dogs in the beginning of the dream? Were they the same who emptied your tank without telling you?"

"I think so. I'm not sure, though. But I believe so."

"What kind of people are they?"

"They're completely self-involved," he answers, irritation sparking in his voice. "They don't care about others. They don't really care about me either. They just want from me. They love my car, not me."

"Laurence borrowed your car when he was here with his lover," I remark.

Christopher looks pained. "They're totally different from Laurence," he replies, tired. "Laurence is vulnerable, tender, and childlike. I can always see the child in him. He's warm. He makes me feel like teaching him, comforting him, protecting him. These people just make me feel disgust. Theirs are just empty words. Laurence is slow to speak, but when he does, it's worthwhile. The only thing they have in common is their optimism. Laurence is sometimes too optimistic, and then he gets gloomy and pessimistic. These characters are always up."

"You feel taken for a ride by them," I say.

"They're a rip-off."

Like the weasel man who charges to the point that Christopher doesn't know if he'll have enough left and may run out at the next crossing.

"What is their life like?"

"They're looking for fun. Fun is all they want. Parties. Constant parties."

"What were you like when you lived that way in the Florida fast lane?"

"Loads of fun," he admits.

"And you feel that kind of life would wear you out. That's at least why you came to me in the first place. To get out of the gay fast lane. Reminds me of the speedboat dream."

I have to go carefully here, because I know of his fundamentalist condemnation of the quest for pleasure. That's what his inner fundamentalist feels AIDS to be a punishment for. But I'm too late. He's already taken my allusions as a punishing judgment and looks dejected.

"So it's because of my life in Florida that I've run out of gas," he mutters, trying to take the slap stoically.

"I believe that you hear me with fundamentalist ears," I try.

"But isn't that what the dream says?" he asks.

"It doesn't give a blanket condemnation of your Florida life," I insist. "It says that the thoughtless, self-absorbed ones lose track of the animal energy and use up your fuel."

"What does that mean?" he asks listlessly.

I'm flustered and feel sweat on my upper lip. I can't seem to think of anything to rescue him from the fundamentalist condemnation. Christopher circles around the hell in which he feels that AIDS is a punishment for his actions in life. I'm sick to my stomach watching him torture himself with instruments I've just unwittingly handed him. Or has my own inner fundamentalist whipped him? I hate myself. Dead end.

△

"I didn't even know what the word *conscript* meant. I had to look it up to make sure. It means someone who's enrolled in the army by compulsion," Christopher declares.

A word picked up unconsciously might still have a flavor of its intended meaning. "So you're involved in a war without having any choice about it," I try.

"Maybe," he ponders.

"Or maybe you've been called on to defend your country now that it is in grave danger from the outside."

"Who knows," he concludes as if it doesn't matter much either way.

9

Christopher has returned from his journey, back to Kansas, Kentucky, and Texas.

"I couldn't make up my mind," he begins. It is May, he's put on some weight, and he's revitalized by his trip to his old homes. He's left with a dilemma, though: should he stay in Boston or go back to Houston? "Now that I'm back here, I'm glad I'm in Boston. But I loved being close to Laurence. And Maggie was darling. She's opened up a part of her house for me. I'd have a beautiful place, and privacy. But somehow I feel I belong here."

I notice that I am very relieved. I would hate him to leave. I'm jealous of his friends in Houston who could pull him away from me. I believe it has to do with my desire to be the great physician who can put the moist vital organ back in. I hear the Magic Healer within me laugh hysterically. I don't particularly like myself at this moment. I also realize that I *need* Christopher to be here. That, I like even less. It is much more comfortable if he's the one in need of me and I can bestow my kind charity upon him.

This is getting messy. I'm aware that I should be careful not to influence his decision.

"I'm glad you're here," I hear my voice say. I feel tricked by myself.

"It's good to see you again, Robert Bosnak," he says with a smile. When he calls me by my full name, he usually tries to inject irony while being sincere at the same time. The warmth between us is palpable. "I couldn't tell Hank," he says quickly.

"You saw him?"

Christopher nods. "In the old age home. He was sitting by

the TV, just like at home. I realized that I was very fond of him. I didn't want to hurt him. So we just talked." He looks sad. "Then, when I left, I thought that I was all alone in the world. That I had literally no one I was related to. I was alone, without a family. I had a conversation with myself: 'What of it? Why do you claim that?' I asked myself. And I answered, 'Because it's true!' Then I asked, 'Or is it because you want it to be true since it makes you less vulnerable?"

"What do you think?"

"I don't know. Maybe I'm keeping myself away from people so I don't have to lose them."

"Did you feel that with Laurence too?"

"A little. But the least of anyone. His vulnerability makes me vulnerable. That's when I wanted to stay in Houston."

"Stay vulnerable, close," I echo.

"I miss Laurence."

I refuse to feel the twang of jealousy I feel in my heart.

"I'm left with a question," he ponders. "I have no family; I'm all alone. How can I be a mature, responsible, caring, related, moral Christian? And gay at the same time. I have no role models anywhere. I don't know if it's even possible." I can see the struggle between his desire to be Christian and his fundamentalist condemnation of himself.

"Have you talked about it with Will?"

"I had a dream about him. Some kind of wish fulfillment probably. I dreamed that Will told me that he was gay. But I know he isn't."

"Did you know that in the dream?"

"No, in the dream I knew he was speaking the truth."

"When did you have this dream?"

"Sunday night. I came back on Saturday and went to church on Sunday. I was impressed by him. It made me less lonely in Boston. I have my friends and all, but I need a Christian community. And Will is a great preacher."

"So you had the dream that night?" He nods. "Where did it take place?" I ask.

"It was in church. But not near the altar. It was in his room.

I've been there several times. It's where we talk. So we were talking. Remember when you told me about the conversation you'd had with that famous Bible scholar?"

I nod. I had told Christopher about a talk I'd had during a conference with a well-known scholar of early Christianity. He had told me that a letter from the second century had been discovered, saying something to the effect that the young disciples came to Jesus at night in his tent, dressed only in sheets, and there he taught them the Kingdom of Heaven. The scholar had been interested in the homosexual connotations of this phrase. We talked about how blasphemous people thought his notions to be. This conversation had always stayed with me, and I relayed it to Christopher at a time when he was brooding about the incompatibility of homosexuality and Christianity. I had said that it may not always have been the case—that in the early church the situation may have been different.

"I asked Will about these young disciples in their sheets. He seemed to know all about that and began to tell me about how common homosexuality had been in the early church. He quoted many books. I was surprised how he could know all these things. So I asked him, 'How come you know all this stuff?' And he answered, 'Christopher, I'm gay.' And I was shocked."

"What did you feel?"

"It was mainly that he said it so completely naturally, as if it were no contradiction at all, being a priest and being gay. Not a tortured thing like with me. That tone of voice shocked me."

"What's the shock like?"

"But I know that Will isn't gay!" Christopher insists, defensively.

"What if he were?"

"But he isn't!"

Wrong tack.

"Forget about that for a moment. Try to feel the shock again."

"It knocks something firm out from under me."

"Some fundament?" I insinuate. I'd love his fundamentalist to become less certain.

"Some kind of belief that I've never doubted."

"What does Will look like at the moment you're shocked?"

"I feel accepted by him. He looks kind."

△

Another orphan dream from the brown corduroy dream book.

Dream 24

Dream of walking by a large body of water, I think the ocean, and come to a place where there is no sand but water comes right to the edge and stops. I put a long willow switch or stick I'm carrying down into it and it is very deep. I think how dangerous it would be for someone to go or fall in there. The area that is like this is about 20 feet long. Then I remember being in a restaurant by the ocean and I'm taking someone's order like a waiter. I'm not very experienced since I can't tell him what goes on a club sandwich. We are watching a storm come in over the water and go by. I have always loved storms and enjoy it.

It strikes me how specific he is in naming the tree from which the measure of depth is taken. It is from a willow tree. The *Dictionary of Symbols and Imagery* by Ad de Vries gives in its first point about the willow tree: "It is generally believed to be a graveside tree, and Odysseus saw willow and black poplar at the entrance of Hades; they grow beside dark Acheron because they need no sunlight." A tree on the verge of the underworld, growing by the river of death. And from that tree Christopher takes the yardstick by which are measured the dangerous depths that swallow the ones who fall into them. Weep, willow, weep.

I have always loved storms and enjoy it. Note that he says this from his position inside the protected place. Looking at the storm, but not being directly exposed to it. On the open ocean, deep beyond belief, he might have been horror-stricken. But Christopher's perspective is sheltered by the nourishing place. The only fallout seems to be a mild confusion. From the point of view of safety, horror becomes fascinating. There is a fundamental difference between the directly experienced overwhelming power of the elements and the aesthetic contemplation of a stormy seascape. At a protective distance the view of a storm can be nourishing, replenishing, and refreshing. Up close, directly exposed, it is the abyss.

△

The next time I see him, I notice that he's been biting his nails. There are even some cuts where it looks as though little wounds have scabbed over. I shake his hand. A few hours later, while I sit with another patient, who has a dream about blood, I realize that Christopher might have had blood on his hands and that I didn't wash my hands after seeing him. Come to think of it, I haven't washed my hands after seeing him since at least a month before he left on his trip. Directly after his return from the hospital, I used to wash my hands meticulously after each time I saw Christopher. After a few weeks it became a ritual, a kind of cleansing. And then, unnoticed, I had stopped, I now realized. I'm surprised. The next time I again "forget" to wash my hands after seeing him. I notice during the hour that I begin to have elaborate pornographic fantasies around drinking his come. Excitement and disgust mix inside my stomach. Then one time I see him, I have an urge to sink my teeth into his pale arm and drink in his blood. Then I realize: *My God, I want to get AIDS!* I'm startled by the unexpected ferocity of my desire to bite him and have our blood mingle.

In the protected surroundings of my study at home I reflect about my relationship with Christopher. I don't realize how my bite is similar to that of his dream rats and dogs, but only feel the unconscious urge to absorb his blood, to fuse with

Christopher. This could become dangerous if I don't become fully aware of it. I instantly feel a profound conviction that it is not because I want to die—not even that I want to die together with him. The depth of our intimacy has led to a longing to become one with him. And the only way to be one with him is to be inside the disease with him. Knowing what he knows, feeling what he feels. I become aware of having indeed noticed that Christopher had some spots of blood on his hands, but I had actively ignored that fact. The next step could be that I would not only ignore his cuts but also "accidentally" cut myself later for our blood to mix. Blood brothers in AIDS. I can now feel the pressure of this passion for fusion and realize that people who work intimately with AIDS patients, or otherwise feel intensely intimate with a person with AIDS might all be exposed to this irrational desire. I should write something about that one day. I look around my room, get up, walk into the kitchen, and see my family—my wife and children, whom I love. I don't want to get AIDS, no way! But the desire to be in a world of AIDS together with Christopher stays put with irrational stubbornness. What doesn't budge, one had better be aware of.

△

From the brown corduroy dream book:

Dream 25

Dream of being in a restaurant like Fridays and I dance with this man. At once I find him very attractive and not my type. We kiss on the floor and it is very deep and passionate. It takes me a moment to come to myself and realize where we are and that we can't do that there. But it is too late. People are already upset and ruckus ensues. I try to avoid it but he seems more a brawler and doesn't particularly mind. He seems like he has to amorize everyone, the women, me, etc. Something seems to have come clear about the difference in trying or wishing to be a

woman and letting her live and be manifest beau-
tifully in a man.

"Friday's is really a restaurant. But this is a kind of dance bar, though it looks like Friday's in Boston. I'm going to bars again. I used to not do it for a while, but now I hang out again. Sometimes someone picks me up. Last week there was this young guy, really attractive." Christopher sees the upset in my face. "Don't worry," he soothes me. "I'm not doing anything dangerous."

"What do you do?"

"Sometimes we masturbate each other. Sometimes I suck someone off. I never endanger anyone!" There is pleading in his voice.

I realize that my inner fundamentalist is convinced that Christopher should remain abstinent for the rest of his life, be forever chaste. I feel a moment of sadistic pleasure in this and am disgusted with myself. Then I look around for the jealousy I'd expect when lovers other than me are mentioned. I don't feel any—not even when I graphically imagine him with another man. Am I like a jealous lover who is so threatened by his jealousy that he can't even feel it?

"Go on," I say.

He looks suspiciously at me for a moment, decides to trust me, and continues. "But most of the time I just hang out there with friends. Or I'm by myself and I carry a notepad to write stuff down in. Since you suggested we write a book together, I've been trying to keep notes." I had made this suggestion after his return from Houston. He would write about his day-to-day experience and I would write about his dream life. "I'd like to write little stories about gay life. So I scribble down ideas, looking at people, seeing things I never noticed before."

"Did you have your notepad with you in the dream?"

"No. The first memory I have in the dream is that I'm sitting at the bar on a stool, sipping a beer, and I see people dance. Men and women. It seems mixed, gay and straight. I shouldn't be drinking." The doctors have told him several

times to avoid alcohol. It has something to do with the drug
AZT and his anemia. Sometimes things get too much for him
and he goes to a bar and drinks a little.

"I see this guy on the dance floor, and the next thing I
know, I'm in his arms dancing. I remember that my first
impression of him was that he's not my type. He has olive
skin and dark curly hair. Just under six foot, I'd say. Round
face."

I try to keep a straight face, noticing that he's giving a
description that sounds just like me. But I remember the
dream about Brendan and the ring, when I asked Christopher
if the ring was like mine, and the massive resistance that
greeted my question. I realized then that our mutual attraction had to remain implicit, never to be mentioned. So I let it
pass. Now I act as if I don't notice, and he pretends not to
notice that I notice and pretend not to notice. The atmosphere crackles with unspoken words.

"Does he look like Peter?" I ask instead, since he had also
said of Peter that he wasn't his type.

"Yes, a little. But this guy is much bigger and stronger.
Peter looked withered. This guy is bursting with vitality. So I
begin to dance with him. We dance real close, and suddenly
we're kissing, kissing passionately. I'm all aflame and I'm
totally involved with the kiss. I'm totally surrounded by the
kiss. I'm inside that kiss. Then suddenly I realize that you
can't do that here. You can't be this sexual here. This is not
the place for it. It's a restaurant. So I break away before
everybody gets angry at me."

I'm thinking about the notion that therapy is not the place
for sex between partners, patient and therapist. This taboo
on literal sex often gets extended to nonphysical sexuality as
well. Christopher is very uncomfortable about the covert
sexual atmosphere, feeling it really shouldn't be. I think of
the sexual dance we're dancing, unspoken, never enacted,
only dreamt.

I have to remind myself that I am not the brawler so I
won't draw Christopher's brawler-energy toward myself,

leaving him to see all that charming vitality in me and unable to feel it as part of his own zest for life. Since the days of Billy, Christopher has always seen this brawny charm in others, unable to recognize it in himself. "How does he respond?" I ask.

"He's gesticulating wildly. Broad gestures. Latin-like. He gets everyone riled up, and he loves it. He thrives on it. He loves a good ruckus. He's having a ball. But he doesn't harm anyone. What I don't understand is that he seems to be charming the pants off of everyone, men and women. They fall for him, and the anger turns to jest. The mood in the place changes. They all love him for his wildness. He's a really wild man. A real man. And at the same time I can see a woman shine from within. And then I have this realization how different he is from the men I know who want to be women. He is a feminine man but in no way effeminate. I'm struck by the fact how different the desire to be a woman is from the capacity to let your inner femininity live freely. I don't know how to describe it better. But I feel that it's crucial."

So do I. As long as Christopher's femininity is locked in the struggle between effeminacy and the hatred of queens, it is torn to shreds, like the peach nightshirt in dream 10, leaving no chance for an interior deepening. Until now, woman was a distant star, longing to be touched, not really human. Now the love for glamorous external beauty has changed in favor of an appreciation of inner beauty. And with the ruin of Christopher's physical self, his new ability to see the value of inner beauty, soul, is indeed crucial. This is the liberation of the inner woman from the shackles of identification with his self-image. Christopher has indeed crossed to the other side to visit Aunt Lib.

△

It is the middle of June. Christopher is pretty much over his great weakness. He's building up strength rapidly. The mood is resilient, close to euphoric. Will's congregation has found the money for Christopher to go to Harvard Extension in the fall to study the psychology of religion, and we dare to feel a measure of optimism. The following experience comes out of the clear blue sky.

"This is not a dream. It happens when I'm sitting in the living room close to the television. The TV is on, but I'm not watching. Suddenly I'm becoming aware of this presence. There's this presence behind me. At first I don't want to turn around. I become very frightened because I realize that the presence behind me is not human. It is something else. I want to get up and leave the room, but I can't move. I concentrate all my energy to try and get up and out of there. Then I remember the times that I've been afraid of dream images— and that I looked at them anyway. I realize that I have to look. So I turn around."

As Christopher says this he begins to actually turn counterclockwise in his chair. I can see a tortured torque going up and down his spine as he rotates against tremendous resistance.

"I can feel him over my left shoulder. And when I'm all turned around I see him." He shudders. "He's about five feet away from me. I'm totally terrified. He looks like the creature from Bald Mountain in Disney's *Fantasia*, or like a huge Darth Vader. He's looking at me. I can just hear his loud breathing." Christopher makes the sound of Darth Vader's breathing: air coming from deep down, forcefully inhaled and exhaled, as through the blowhole of a sea mammal. I can feel the creature come into the room because he's so alive in Christopher at this moment. I get goose bumps and am struck with terror.

"I look at him, and he is so dark. Darker than night. Black emptiness. But not formless. He is enshrouded in some kind of cape made of scales, like a dragon or a giant serpent. I notice that I'm shaking, and I realize that I'm terrified like I've never been in my life. I press my eyes shut, hoping it will go away. But it doesn't. When I open my eyes, he's right in front of me again.

"Then suddenly I know: this is the Spectre of Aids! I know that I've been trying not to relate to Aids at all. But now I must face Aids. I keep looking at him. I notice his scales, and I'm terrified. I feel dark through and through. Dark and forsaken.

"Then I cried. When I stopped crying he had gone. For several days it went like that. I would be sitting in the living room and he would come. But it was different, because I invited him. Somehow that made me less scared of him. But it didn't change the terror I felt. Then yesterday he comes again. I sit there looking at him and he at me, though I couldn't see his eyes. I see his reptilian scales. I feel freezing cold, looking at this Angel of Darkness. Then, very rapidly, I have three memories. First I remember how Satan comes disguised as an angel of light. Then I remember a picture by William Blake of a father image who had cloven hoofs and a serpentine body and who came to frighten and terrify. And finally Christ as serpent in the wilderness.

"Then I have a very sharp insight: Jesus was called not only to overcome the childish fear of waking up in the middle of the night, but to go in and redeem hell itself, when the face is truly turned away. I know that to really love God, I have to love Him when His face is averted. When He comes to me in apparent darkness. I wouldn't truly love Him if I only wanted His light. With this insight, something has changed about the spectre. I begin to see light. The light is coming from behind the scaly mantle. He is opening up his mantle, and I see eyes, thousands of eyes looking at me. I know that these are the eyes of the Shekhina, the female aspect of God dwelling in the world. The light is magnificent, and I feel seen. I feel totally seen. And I feel love."

We're silent for a long moment.

"I wrote it down," he says finally.

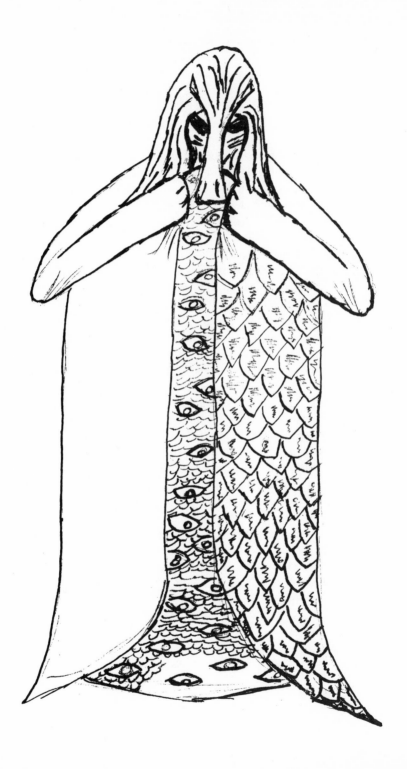

The Spectre of Aids

At first is something more felt or sensed than related to: a sense of dealing with something as impersonal as to be called a spectre. It was like some huge, hot thing breathing down my neck standing behind me. I don't want to relate to AIDS at all, but I know I must. Feeling the inadequacy of a mortal trying to relate to a god that I do not trust cares for me.

In the first couple of relatings he was silent, totally black, enshrouded in his black cape which was scaly. He is the embodiment of sinister purpose or evil and darkness—fear and death.

The image I see is like the creature from Bald Mountain in Disney's Fantasia. At this point I realize God's presence in all things. If, as the scripture says, Satan comes disguised as an angel of light, why cannot God come disguised as an angel of darkness? I then remember the image of Christ himself depicted as a brazen serpent. I start to allow for there to be light in the darkness. Darkness and light and shadow become a matter of where the light source is placed.

I see that if I love you and to get the needed response or movement I have to confront you with apparent darkness, it would be less than loving to soften it, make it less scary. I must do and present what it takes. The dark frightening spectre becomes lightbringer.

The final exchanges show him beginning to open his cape and inside is spectacular light and eyes associated with Shekhina or God-presence. The Spectre is an old friend to whom day and night are both alike: his frightening disguise coming to me as perfect love and terrible.

I'm struck by the fact that he writes the name of the disease as a personal name, no longer as an impersonal acronym—

Aids, not AIDS. Aids has become an Other with whom Christopher has begun to communicate.

"I also drew a picture of the spectre." He hands it to me. "I didn't have the energy to draw in all the scales and all the eyes," he mentions apologetically. I look at the drawing for a long time, trying to feel the spectre's presence. Then I put it down on the little round table beside us. I flip the paper over, so as not to be distracted by the drawing. On the back there is writing in pencil. It says:

feminine voices of God

10

While working on this book I am plagued with the notion that Christopher has become a fictional character.

What I have set out to do is to re-create my intimate encounter with Christopher. I try to bring back the moods and atmospheres between us, varying from conscious to mutually unconscious feelings. Intimacy is foremost a play of feelings. I try therefore to make Christopher as alive as I remember him. I don't give a so-called verbatim report, except for the complete text of the brown corduroy dream book. I try to describe the intimacy Christopher and I share. That is where the interior combustion of our relationship takes place.

But the voice in me that says "This is not at all the way it was!" remains strong. What it was is lost. I just know what it is. This is the problem with the entire literary genre called "case history." It purports to describe reality-as-it-really-is, while in fact it describes the memory of the author. In my case, a visual memory of the images returns to me when I read over Christopher's dreams again. I hear our discussions once more; it calls back the atmosphere and finally Christopher himself. His dream book is my anchor.

△

The brown corduroy dream book contains entries referring to the searches Christopher goes on and the talks we have over the ensuing weeks:

—*Body's symptoms as characters to be related to or organic symptomatizing*

Now that I've actually seen Aids in person, my

relationship to Aids has changed. If you see the symptoms of the body as characters, illness is different from just seeing it as a heap of organic symptoms. It has become a "Thou," an Other you can communicate with. . . .

—journey from "it" to "thou" by the "justs"

This feeling that it is "just physical" obstructs me. I have to get by this barrier to get from the world as an "it" to the world as a "Thou." It sets up a world of communion. . . .

—Outer relationships reflecting inner realities projected

And if I can't feel the world as Other inside my own self, I can't really communicate with people. I will see people as objects, like I've always seen myself as an object.

—Dissociated components desire to be real-ized. Relating to them realizes them.

I had split off Aids from myself. Pushed it away. That gives everything a sense of unreality. Now that I know that I'm with Aids and have begun relating to Aids, my world is suddenly real again.

—the grand disguise: would you love me and trust me and pursue me if I looked like pain and evil?

It is easy to love God when His face is loving and light. It is essential to me that I know that it's God who's presenting Himself in the guise of pain, looking evil. It stretches my love for Him and for people. He's no longer silent. I understand that he'd been silent because I hadn't looked in his direction.

—good-evil polarity as a construct rather than a response quality

What seems to be split like night and day isn't really. It's my response that makes it so. If I respond to my terror as to someone terrified and see the terror as a real being, it stops being just evil.

—the degree to which we will go to escape pain, death and love

The following entries were not discussed, and I pass them along with only a few comments. Some headings are self-evident, others shrouded in incomprehensibility.

—calling the child to account and maturity through projection and faith

—Trinity or quaternity of Godhead a model for individuation or what is needed to love, minister and create.

The word *individuation* alludes to an ancient concept stating that every creature in its unfolding will manifest according to its innate form. A chicken's egg will not produce a dog. C. G. Jung took this concept and ran with it in a psychological direction, intending it to mean the process of the unfolding of one's interior blueprint—as our inborn selfhood gets molded by and molds our environment. Jung alludes to emergence of the integral wholeness of the human being, the total form of being human. The entire spectrum of our interior selves spans the most undifferentiated and impersonal realms of psyche, where masculine and feminine are indistinguishable, as well as the most specific and personal shape of one's idiosyncratic individuality. Since wholeness is usually imagined by the number four and by the circle—the four quarters of the earth, the four seasons of the year, the mandala—Jung refers to the quaternity (based on a four-partite system) as an image of wholeness and to the Trinity (based on the number three), the basis of Christianity, as lacking wholeness since it has excluded the feminine. (Virgin-Mother Mary is not part of the Trinity.) Christopher is well aware of this.

—2010 with its two suns would indeed make it more difficult to decide where was shadow and where light. Could the appearance of shadow only be a statement of perspective and where one places the light? Does it then seem so odd that day and night be alike to One dwelling in light? Are we called to be the light set on the hill, the light of the world? Jesus was called not only to overcome the childish fear of walking into the night but to go in and redeem Hell itself when the face is truly turned away.

—Why do most seem to live in relative ease, without trauma as their "life"?

—We are Legion, full of the devil, disembodied spirits needing to be embraced and made real light

Maybe "real light" refers to the inclusion of the searing and the tortured colors in one's spectrum. Is it the nature of all light that it wants to be seen? Christopher's face had been averted just as much as his God's.

Dream 26

Dream of being in the home we had growing up: a huge 130 year old house. Apparently it is time for a Christmas tree and Ethel has brought home this odd pole like tree and wants it upstairs instead of in the reception hall stairway area. Because we have nearly always had the huge trees I wanted I agree though I'd rather have a big tree again and downstairs. It seems odd to me that they are not using the whole house. Later I walk into a room and Laurence is there and we have sex.

"The landscape around my home is like in the movie *Return to Bountiful*. I saw that film right after returning from my trip back home, and I cried all the way through, thinking of going back home. The fields, the houses, the village she passed through on her way home, that was like my home." His voice weeps with nostalgia; his eyes are dry. "I could so much feel the longing of that old woman to see her hometown once more."

I can see the street and the canal in the back of my Dutch childhood home. I long for my neighbor girl and our first kisses. We've entered the land of homesickness.

"The house is white Victorian, a little run down, in a field sloping down around it." Like a Wyeth painting, I think to myself. "I'm inside. It is mainly brown inside. I'm in the hall near the stairway. High ceilings. I'm my present age. We stand by the stairs, Hank and I, when Ethel enters with the Christmas tree. Hank makes some funny remarks about the tree, how scrawny it is. I free up a space around the place where we usually put the tree. I'm sad that it's such a sickly little pole instead of one of those magnificent trees Ethel used to bring home. But Ethel motions upstairs. That's a second shock. I want the tree where it has always been, but it gets kicked upstairs." We smile at each other, acknowledging the pun.

"Ethel brings the tree up the stairs. She's holding the tree in one hand. It's really small, almost a bald pole. I stand in the corner of the hall, at the place where we used to celebrate Christmas. I see the tree going upstairs in Ethel's hand. I feel a sudden longing for Christmas as it used to be, when I was a child, with the big tree and all the presents under it." I have a quick flash of the "Christmas room" and the old dessert lady (dream 10).

"I've always loved the lights and the beautiful Christmas ornaments. I still have three. Two balls of very thin glass. Beautiful. Handmade. They came from when Ethel was a child. There was a star too." A star, I hear, thinking of Marilyn-Earth Mother and of Ethel, who carries the tree to a higher story. "I sometimes just take them out and look at them. They're very frail and beautiful. And so is my memory of the Christmases of my childhood. I remember the lights. Many lights. Then I realize that Ethel has always given me everything I wanted. When I wanted the big trees as a kid, she gave me the big trees. So I had to accept what she gave us this time for Christmas."

"How does it feel to have to accept that?"

"It goes against the grain at first. I so much want a big tree! It is a deep longing. Just as much as having Christmas downstairs and not upstairs."

"You prefer a full-bodied celebration down here, where you've always had it, to a scrawny celebration upstairs." I conclude to make him hear his own words with metaphoric overtones.

"But I have to agree with Ethel," he says with an expression in his face that indicates that he's hearing his own words on several levels. "I have to give in because she has always been so generous to me."

"Is it because it wouldn't be fair to contest it? Is it like submitting to some kind of sense of justice?"

He nods. "Yes. But it hurts. I'd so much want a huge tree down here."

△

"The house is so much bigger than I thought. I roam from room to room. So many rooms are unoccupied. They live just in such a small part of the house. It is strange that they don't use all the rooms they have."

"Like they hardly know their own place?"

"Maybe they know it, but they're certainly not using it. I don't get it. It's such a big house, and they're living as if they were in a tiny apartment. They did use the living room off the hall most. That's where Hank hung out in front of the TV and where Ethel would do her chores. But in the dream it is much more disproportionate. They're hardly using any of the house, and it's much larger than what I remember."

"Do you see it from the height of a child, maybe?"

"No, it has many more rooms. I keep on opening doors to rooms."

"What are the empty rooms like?"

"Some look like there has never been anything in them;

they've always been unused. Others have been uninhabited for a long time. They all feel like wasted space."

I think of a tract of land where we used to play soccer, near the last stop of the streetcar, where it turns around to go the other way. I think of all the life I have forgotten and about Christopher withering, musing about all the rooms he could have inhabited. The nostalgia is palpable. *I have wasted my life,* I hear Christopher's words echo.

Our silence lasts minutes. Unspoken words speak eloquently.

"What is the room like in which you meet Laurence?" I ask.

The mood breaks instantly. Christopher smiles broadly, very relieved. "It's a bare room with a double bed. Just a white sheet on the bed. That's all there is in the room. Just Laurence and a bed. That's all I want." He smiles with a flush of shyness. I feel a pang of jealousy and know how at this very moment Christopher loves Laurence to the exclusion of anyone else. Laurence on the bed is the love of his life. Laurence is life itself. All of Christopher's love for life gushes hotly toward Laurence.

The empty wasteland and the spring of life alternate in rapid succession.

Dream 27

Dream of being I think somewhere in Texas. Felt like I was a guest. One of the men suggests that he would enjoy borrowing my rented convertible about which I am reticent. It also becomes apparent that I have agreed to take care of a baby, I think mine and I think black. The women have always had to take care of it and though I don't seem prepared to do so, it seems right.

"It was very much like when I was in Texas six weeks ago. I felt like a guest. I knew that I didn't live there anymore. I felt like a guest with everyone I was with. With Laurence, with Maggie. I loved to be with them. And it was wonderful how they all took care of me. But I was their guest. I didn't live there anymore. I live in Boston now."

I feel both relief at the prospect that Christopher is going to stay with me and sadness when I think of my friends in Holland and how I live in America now. "Does that make you sad?" I ask.

"Yes, even though I'm glad to be in Boston."

"Was the man who wanted to borrow your convertible similar to—"

"My Florida friends who borrowed my convertible in the other dream? Yes, he was. He was just like them." We smile at each other, enjoying our flash of apparent telepathy.

"Why do you think it was rented?" I wonder out loud.

"Because I was there just for a visit. I lived somewhere far away. So I had my own car somewhere else."

Maybe he just has a short lease on the fast lane, I think to myself. He looks better than he's looked since he got Aids. He just had a blood transfusion. His T-cell count is up; AZT seems to do its work. That's good. We look to the T-cell count as a barometer for his atmospheric pressure: if it goes down we feel life heavier than if it's up. If it's up, it means he can fight off the dangerous viral intruders.

His skin is very dry and slightly scaly in places. But his old green convertible is parked across the street with the roof down and the sun is shining. It's summertime and the living is easy—which leads me to the black baby. Being on the fast track sounds very different from taking care of a baby.

"Tell me about the black baby," I request.

"It's vague. I'm pretty sure it's black, and I remember women in a room."

"What kind of room?"

"Something round, maybe?" There's an audible question curve in his tone.

"You mean a round room?"

"Maybe, yes. But it is really vague. I don't know."

I can feel the image slipping. "Anything that stands out?" I ask quickly.

"Someone, a woman, hands me the baby. I can feel the baby."

"Try and feel your arms," I ask, responding to the feeling near my heart of rocking a baby in my arms.

"My arms are warm. I'm often cold, even when the sun is out. It feels good that my arms are warm. That's how I feel when she gives me the baby. I feel warm. That's why I know it's right even though I feel absolutely unprepared. And that's how I know it's my baby."

"What does it feel like to hold your baby?"

"It's a beautiful baby. I love black babies. They're beautiful."

I remember our talking about black babies and how for Christopher black people are related to the ability to feel deeply. The depth of interior blackness is now his own beautiful baby, making him warm all over.

When I asked him to write down a list under the heading "Nigger," at the top of it were the names of Kunte and Kizzie. I never got a chance to ask him about them. And now that I see the list he made of his male and female images, there they are again—now prominently at the bottom of the list, after Ethel, Mae West, Nan, Marlene Dietrich, Maggie, John Gielgud, William Hurt, Tom Cruise, John, Billy, and Laurence. I don't remember who they are. They might have been characters from Alex Haley's novel *Roots*. I don't know. I wish I could say at this point that I continued by asking about Kunte and Kizzie, but I didn't. They slipped by me like people you don't know and therefore don't see. Maybe because of the distance between Holland and Kentucky I didn't fathom their importance. My hometown wasn't Bountiful.

"Can you concentrate on holding the black baby?"

He closes his eyes.

"What do you feel?"

"Warm."

"Anything else?"

"It's mine."

"Like the fish child?"

He nods. "I feel exactly as protective as then. He feels very vulnerable in my arms. I want nothing to happen to him. He feels like he's part of me. He's flesh of my flesh."

"You're nervous?"

"Well, I don't particularly know how to take care of babies. I'm kind of fidgety. Just trying not to drop the baby. I remember thinking something about diapers and feeling a short moment of panic." He grins broadly. "But the feeling that he's mine is much stronger."

"He?"

"I don't know. Just because you said Fish Child, I suppose. I really don't remember. And anyway, it doesn't really matter."

"If it doesn't really matter, could it be that the baby is both male and female?" I try.

"I don't think so. It was one or the other. But he was basically human."

"Black human."

"Yes. It's a beautiful baby."

We hold the silence to let the feeling sink in.

"How is it for you that a black preacher has found the money for your studies in psychology and religion at Harvard Extension?" It's a question I've long wanted to ask, but the occasion never presented itself.

"Very unexpected. I'd never thought I'd be helped financially by blacks."

"It must throw your racist and his nigger for a loop."

"My racist doesn't believe that Will is going to come up with the money. 'I'll be surprised when I see the actual check,' he says. The racist is very cynical about it all."

I hope that the baby prefigures a sense of the underlying sameness of all humans. That would make the frighteningly Other more similar. It might deepen the love of sameness, the homo-eros. I ponder about the relationship between racism and homophobia. Hating other races in fear of their sameness to us. I drift off in thoughts.

"I can feel the love blacks have for their children. It's very deep," Christopher says with a trace of awe.

△

From the brown corduroy dream book.

Dream 28

Dream of wanting to go to "the house," think my
uncle Jimmy's house I used to stay the summers when
a child. Was going to cut across a field but can't
because of one of the two horses in the field. One is
nice and the other is aggressive and threatening.
Walk away from there and up toward barn. Decide
some milkweeds need burning away on the field.
Become afraid barn is going to catch afire. One corner
seems hot.

"What is milkweed?" I ask, never sure of names of plants
in English. "Does it have anything to do with milk?"
"Yes. It produces some kind of milky juice. Like thin milk.
It has those long pods that open up and have tufts of white
spores inside that fly all over, like when you tear open a down
pillow and shake it. That's why you have to do something
about it, 'cause it spreads like anything."
"Is the juice that comes out of the weeds similar to the sap
that rises when you're making love with the young man in
the aquarium with Ava looking on?" (dream 17), I ask,
feeling a connection between those dreams.
"A little. Milkweed juice is a little whiter, but it's more or
less the same. Why?"
"Because of the burning of the juices," I respond cryp-
tically. He doesn't understand. Neither do I. "With the dream
in the aquarium the juices were beginning to rise again after
the moist vital organ had been removed, right?" I try again.
He nods. "This is an image of the burning of the juicy weed,
that's all. To control the weed from spreading, you burn the
juices."
"Sounds like AZT," he says. "I just got a blood transfusion
because the AZT gives me anemia. Do you mean that?"

"I hadn't thought of that," I admit. "But it sure sounds similar. I was thinking more along the lines of the juices that get flowing and the juices that dry up. It felt to me that the juices got flowing when you were holding the baby. It made you all warm inside."

"And you mean that now I'm drying up again?" he asks, worried.

"I don't believe things change that much from one moment to the next. You had the dreams within a few days of each other. It seems more as if it is all happening at the same time: the juicing and feeling warm all over; and the burning and drying and feeling ice-cold. I've got no idea what it means."

He shrugs his shoulders and stares off somewhere.

I get nervous and become more interpretive. "Like the two horses. There are two horses in the field. Two kinds of energies, two forms of horse power." I notice that I must be close to panic because my interpretations are becoming rote: this-means-that. "One horse power is nice, nice energy. The other is threatening, aggressive, destructive energy. And they're in the same field."

He nods, clearly not caring what I'm talking about. I give up.

Silence.

"Who is Uncle Jimmy?" I ask to get his interest going again.

"I'm tired," he says. He suddenly looks exhausted.

"You feel burnt out?" I ask.

He nods.

I'm afraid the barn has already caught fire.

11

From the brown corduroy dream book.

Dream 29

In a suburban setting—hot, Texas like. Am dressed in shorts and pattern shirt—orange and red. Decide to go I think to the bookstore but need shoes and more money which are at home. In next scene I'm riding a very expensive bicycle I hopped on from someone's house. A very fancy house and obviously rich—Suddenly I realize that I have stolen the bike and take it back. When I have replaced it I'm talking to the father of the house and he's showing me what all the "bike" can do. It has changed appearance and upon pushing a latch the front section comes loose and is a yard roller—the kind one would fill with water to roll lumps out of the lawn. Only instead of rolling the lawn, we are now in the house and he rolls it across the couch and carpet as if cleaning them (and they do look a little dirty) Blue and white interior. I have the feeling it's their son I've been involved with.

"Everything about the interior is blue and white. The couch is a pale marine blue and the carpet is white. You can see every spot on it. I'm at first surprised that the roller doesn't crush the couch. It's very heavy and puts on a lot of pressure. But somehow it cleans things very well. It is also surprising that he's using it inside."

This is all we got a chance to say about his dream. It fell in between the cracks of daily events. Christopher has found a job in an elegant boutique owned by a friend. He gets paid by the hour, and he can come and go when he pleases. His friends take good care of him. He tells about someone who, when it was found out that he had Aids, was kicked out of his home by his roommates, lost his job, and became destitute. We talk about the idea of his meeting other people with Aids, but Christopher refuses. "I get life from the living," he keeps repeating. A church group has asked him to speak and a television reporter, moved by his spirit, invites him for an interview on her TV show. A young man at the bar has become so enamored of Christopher—who no longer looks emaciated, just thin—that Christopher is all flustered, not knowing what reason to give the young man for not having intercourse with him. He doesn't want to admit that he has Aids. Before it becomes a serious problem, though, the love cools, but it leaves Christopher with a heightened self-esteem, knowing that he's still attractive.

Christopher is hot, riding high on an expansive cycle. But this cycle is stolen and has to be returned to the Father, who proceeds to transform it into a cycle of heavy downward pressure that cleanses the interior. The cleaning cycle of the Father—whom Christopher knows through his love for the Son—is designed to flatten the ground of being by applying the gravity of water. In the exterior cycle of the fast lane, life's juices are used for propulsion. In the interior cycle they become a crushing weight that cleanses.

From the brown corduroy dream book.

Dream 30

Dream of travelling with Hank and Ethel on an extended trip with multiple sections or legs. Part was by helicopter which I had to fly and didn't really know how. Then I remember driving long and tiring parts. One incident was when Ethel was driving and I realize we were going 100 and that she was asleep. I got very angry and made her let me drive. She suggested I should have been watching. Later somewhere we stopped for gas. I am enraged when one of

*the small children throws orange juice in the back of
the car (a station wagon). I go in and tell the owner
of the store that I think the child should be spanked
and preach that that is how I learned to respect the
property of others.*

"Everything is vague up to the moment that Ethel is asleep
behind the wheel at a hundred miles an hour. Before that I
remember the chopper. Not being able to fly it. Being afraid
of crashing. But it doesn't have much detail to it. I can clearly
see Ethel. Her seat is back, her head is tilted to one side. I see
the landscape zoom by and the speedometer way over to the
right. I get furious. Hank is in the back. He's asleep too. It has
been a very exhausting trip. I can feel that I'm tired also. But
that doesn't make me any less angry at Ethel.

"I grab the wheel and bring the car to a stop. She wakes up
and doesn't want me to do the driving. I just push her over
and say that it's much too dangerous like this—that she has
no sense of responsibility. I yell at her. Hank doesn't wake up.
She's very cynical, saying that it was my responsibility just as
much as hers. We were on this trip together, and I should
have been well aware of how dangerous it was. That these
long drives wear you out. I can't just assume that she'd drive
and I could rest. That makes me even more angry. I push her
off the driver's seat and drive on.

"I notice that we're almost out of gas. I tell her, but she
doesn't listen. I'm extremely annoyed. I pull over on some
country road at an old gas station. The building is white. It is
self-service, and I fill up the tank. It had been almost
completely empty. Then I go in to pay. I notice a group of
little black kids playing around. It's in the South somewhere. I
pay, and when I come out I see one of the youngest of the
kids, maybe five years old, throw this whole container of
orange juice into the back of the station wagon. Everything
will be a sticky mess, and I am beside myself. I first debate
whether or not to give the kid a spanking but decide against it
because I don't know how the people around would react. I
run back inside and tell the owner about the incident. I'm all

109

fired up with indignation and say that the kids should be punished. A good spanking would help. Kids should learn to respect the property of others. I used to get spanked; that's how you learn. I notice that I sound like a preacher."

"Can you feel how exhausting the trip has been?" I ask.

"It just seems to keep on going. One trip after the next. It basically seems to be several trips. After each trip I'm more tired."

"Can you feel the exhaustion right now?"

"I feel it all the time. It is always there."

"Where do you feel it in your body?"

"In my chest, mainly." He looks apprehensive. The fear of pneumocystis twists his face. For a moment I think I see through to his skull. I remember the little weasel man who charges too much so that Christopher will not have enough for the next crossing. Each trip is more exhausting than the previous one. More running on empty.

"Does it feel as if life is just zipping by without your having any grip on it, so you can hardly catch your breath?" I say, trying to give a metaphoric twist to the unconscious speed in the dream.

"Maybe. But it's more that it's slipping through my fingers and that I want to live as much as I can. But then I get so tired." He slumps. I wait, feeling a cough come up from the depth of my lungs. Then I cough as if I've just swallowed food down the wrong pipe. Christopher looks startled.

"Are you all right?" he asks, concerned.

I nod, tears in my eyes. His concern is very warm and genuine. I feel tired. I work too much, see too many people. I feel a pain in my chest. Christopher looks at me, worried. It must be disconcerting to have a hysteric who unconsciously mimics your symptoms for an analyst. I feel ridiculous.

"How is it to fly a helicopter?" I ask after I've caught my breath.

"I was frightened as hell. It's even more frightening than being in a plane you can't fly. With a plane you have the feeling that at least you've got wings holding you up. But with a chopper there's nothing!"

"Do you fall out of the sky?"

"No. Somehow I fly it. I don't crash. I don't know how, but it stays up." He sounds frightened.

"So you're not chopped by the chopper." I grin. The moment of fear breaks.

"I'm not yet dead meat, if that's what you mean," he quips.

There's a parallel with the dream about putting raw hamburger meat behind the tire of a van (dream 10). I don't notice it.

"So your memory becomes clear at the point where Ethel is asleep in the fast lane," I say, trying to make a connection to the Florida fast guys who also made him run out of gas.

"She's actually snoring; that's the first thing I remember." His face is glowing with humor. I laugh. "She's snoring so loud that it woke me up. And then I look out and see the car going faster than it's ever gone before, and on my left is Ethel, whose snoring is all I hear."

"The view is of speed and the sound is of snoring?" I ask, to underline the fact of this simultaneity. He nods.

"So the speed and the sleep are parts of each other," I ponder out loud.

Hoping for an interpretation, he waits for me to go on with my contemplations. I have nothing further to say, but I feel a pressure to say something.

"When Ethel has no consciousness left, then the speed becomes manic," I try.

Christopher nods without understanding.

"Who's Ethel?" I ask.

Now he looks annoyed, as if I had huge holes in my memory.

"What is the first thing that comes to your mind when you hear the name Ethel?" I clarify.

He looks relieved. "She takes care of me," he says without hesitation.

"So it is the faculty that can take care of you that's asleep. There's no one taking care of you, that *is* the speed. That's like the tension in the dream a few sessions ago between the speed freak who wants to take the convertible for a spin and the one who takes care of the baby. It seems that you have to take care of Christopher. And if you remain asleep, you can't do it," I conclude, addressing the caring faculty directly.

He looks lost in thought.

"It reminds me of Peter, who was behind you in the Marilyn dream. He was deeply unconscious. That's how he'd almost died, because of his unconscious love life. And Marilyn-Earth Mother is the one who cares for Peter. If she doesn't care, no one will."

"You mean that Ethel and Earth Mother are alike?"

"I don't know." I evade for reasons that I truly don't know and also because I want to put as little emphasis as possible on a potential similarity between these two figures. The sense of connection mustn't exceed the level of a fleeting hunch. If similarity is too heavily emphasized, it becomes identity, and only one synthetic image remains from the two you have before. You lose differentiation.

"You're a great help." He grins and his eyes twinkle.

"Ethel gets angry with you?" I ask, returning his grin.

"Yes. She says that I'm just as responsible as she is."

"She doesn't want you to behave like a trusting child. You have to be awake yourself. You can't just blindly trust Mother anymore; you have to keep your eye on her. You've got to be on guard."

"That's one of the things that wears me out. That I've always got to be on guard. Anything can kill me."

"Is it like you can't just take your body for granted anymore, that you have to be watchful all the time?" I ask, feeling drained. "It feels to me like being in a permanent state of siege," I add, feeling my backbone slump.

Christopher smiles faintly. He looks so endlessly tired.

The atmosphere becomes drowsy. To avoid our falling asleep, I ask him about the last section of the dream.

"It's the youngest of the kids who does it. He is lugging this big container of orange juice. He's five or maybe seven.

Nobody is paying any attention to him. The carton is almost too big for him to lug. It's at least a gallon. I see him walking to the back of the car when I come out of the store where I've paid. I see him approach the car, and I believe that he's just going to peek inside. He's very small and very black. I think he's cute. Then he suddenly swings the carton and hurls the O.J. into the open window of the station wagon."

"What do you feel at that moment?"

"I'm astonished. It's the last thing I'd expected. At first I'm not even angry, only shocked. I just stand there not believing my eyes. Then I get furious. I first want to run up to him and give him a good spanking. But I don't want to create a riot, so I turn around instead to tell the owner."

"Is the owner black also?"

"No, the owner is white."

"So then you give your tirade?"

"Yes. I talk very loud. I can see the black kids with their noses pressed against the store window. Laughing faces. That makes me even more livid."

"What does your voice sound like?"

"It's loud. I don't know how to describe it."

"Can you do it for me?"

"I'll try," he says hesitantly. Christopher closes his eyes and waits for a moment. Suddenly he bursts out in a brimstone-and-damnation voice that shakes the high pulpit he stands on. "He should learn that he can't do a thing like that. He should know to respect property of others. He should be spanked as an example to all the others that we will not tolerate such mischief. I learned to change my ways when I was spanked after misbehaving. We should set an example." He's all fired up.

"What do you sound like?"

"Like the kind of preacher I can't stand. I preach principle. It has nothing to do with that little boy anymore. I'm in a state of righteous anger."

"Feel the righteousness."

"It's more self-righteous than anything else. It fills me

with a sense of truth beyond all doubt. It makes me feel strong."

"It sounds old to me," I comment, feeling pushed away and very young.

"Old and wise."

"More like old and rigid," I insist. "It feels like dry bones to me. No moisture, no flexibility. And as if you have no shadow. You're a scorching light, and the little black boy is a pitch-black shadow. You're all good and he's all bad." I feel glee and notice that I'm beginning to sound like a punishing preacher myself. I remember his Florida shoplifting and am full of condemnation.

Christopher looks ashamed. I seem to have hit something. I feel triumph. The preacher is very aggressive, glad to have found a righteous cause to lash out at. At the same time I feel ashamed of myself. We sit in the shame together.

"Sometimes I get very preachy," I say apologetically, "It is one of my pitfalls in analysis." Christopher doesn't understand what I'm talking about. He looks puzzled. "Being like a rigid priest is not just your problem," I explain. We look eye to eye, feeling intimate.

"Maybe we just don't understand what the black boy is doing," I continue after some time. "Tell me your associations about O.J."

"I can't wake up if I don't have a glass of O.J. in the morning," he says without hesitating. "It's even more important to me than coffee. It feels as if I'm doing something healthy for myself." His voice trails off in thought.

"Waking you up; healthy," I repeat. Christopher nods. "And you need waking up," I add. "Ethel falls asleep behind the wheel. You could use some pepper up your ass," I quip coarsely, to bring to life the image of the wake-up juice thrown into the back of the car. "Pepper up your rear" is a Dutch expression meaning bubbling over with vitality. I hope it has similar reverberations in English; folk expressions often do. "What do you make of it that the juice enters from behind?" I ask.

"Do you mean sexually?" he responds.

"Whatever comes to mind," I evade.

"You mean that I wanted men inside me?"

I don't answer.

"It did make me feel very alive to have a man inside me. But this is a little kid! I've never had anything to do with little kids." He looks offended.

"I know," I soothe him in a gentle voice, "But look at it through the eyes of the little boy. You said that no one paid any attention to him. Maybe he wants someone to pay attention to him."

"You mean that no one cares for him?"

I nod. "Try to feel like that little boy that nobody pays attention to."

"I'm angry," he says after a while. "I'm angry that no one cares a damn about me. I just want them to pay attention. I'll make a mess of their clean car. I'm very angry." Christopher sounds surprised at the intensity of the anger he's expressing. He's really pissed. I wonder if the little black boy had a gallon's worth of being pissed. We're silent while the anger works its way through his system until it calms down.

"Maybe the little black kid has to do with those vital deep feelings you feel blacks have. Without them you feel empty, just roaming around aimlessly." I feel off. I'm manipulating him toward an answer I have preconceived. But I want him to come up with it himself. It's about his anality. His passion for cleanliness. I keep on buggering him with it. I try to sneak up from behind to make my insight penetrate him. He looks confused. I want him to make the connection between the clean wagon before the infusion of the black boy's juices and the sticky mess afterward. His horror of messes came up before, when we talked about the house of Nan where the unruly animals made a mess. And in the dream of the printmaker who made a mess downstairs. We had talked about how extremely clean he wants his home to be, already long before this became a necessity because of Aids. His cleanliness is compulsive. Freud says that orderliness, parsimoniousness, and obstinacy go together and are related to the dissipation of anal-erotism, making for the anal character. But how can I get that across? My urge to penetrate him makes me aggressive.

"You can't stand it that your car gets dirty," I exclaim bluntly.

"What would you do if someone threw orange juice into your car?" he asks quietly.

"I mean that you always want things meticulously clean," I clarify.

"You're trying to tell me I'm anal." He grins, as if it were a matter of course. My precious insight suddenly looks banal to me.

△

It is late July. The sun is out and Christopher invites me over to his home to spend an evening with him and his roommate, John. He is eagerly awaiting my answer, having a blush on his otherwise pale face. I'm in a quandary.

"I can understand if you couldn't come," he adds generously, making his invitation harder to refuse.

I don't want to be like regular friends with him. I feel it's important to confine our time together to the hours when we meet in my office. I'm very clear about that. The reason why I have this certainty is less tangible. It probably is because I don't want him flooding my life. And I assure myself that it is bad analytical practice to have your patients take you home. I sound bookish to myself. It is probably all a defense. But the certainty is no less firm.

"I would love to," I begin.

"We could have long talks!" he interrupts joyously.

I immediately feel overburdened. Everything is getting too much for me. I need a vacation. This is getting out of hand. Get me out of here! I don't have the time. I feel like the jeweler who doesn't want Christopher to come work for her back home in Houston. I have no time for him. I'm just before my August break and I'm holding on by my fingernails.

▲

"Maybe," I agree, cowardly. I see his hopes rising. He looks very satisfied. I hate to disappoint him. But the weight on my shoulders increases and my chest collapses further.

"I would love to, but I can't," I can't help saying.
He looks disappointed.
I don't have the energy. Not even the energy to say that I don't have the energy.
Thank God for August.

12

A dreamless summer break.

When I return in September, Christopher tells me of beaches around Boston and of fleeting, careful nightly romance. And he tells how friends he never knew he had are coming to speak with him about their problems.

"I listen to them. Their stories sound so alike. Everyone seems to have trouble with his partner. Everyone seems to be afraid of getting old. But they are open to me. They feel that I can understand them. I have a friend who's blind, whom I love. We have these long conversations, walking down the beach. I took him in my car. He lives with his mother and has to wait for people to take him. But there's always someone. He's so gentle, and so loyal! Last December he sat with me in the hospital for days on end. But the others—they all seem to be searching. And I'm going around in bars to see the scene and write. I see how people are searching for security, frightened of getting older. There's nothing more pathetic than an old faggot trying to look young. It makes me sad. So I talk with my friends about shadow. About the fear of the dark, outside and inside."

He seems to love the attention and respect others give him.

I feel relieved, because I had been a bit apprehensive about my one-month break, when I leave my practice behind clouds of oblivion to refuel. I can't even feign that I've missed him, because I haven't. I hesitate to talk about it, out of guilt for my vacation to health and self-involvement.

"I didn't miss you much," he volunteers an answer to my unspoken question.

"I'm glad," I reply with a pang of regret. But I don't want to deal with it any further. Every September feels like I'm pushing a heavy rock up a hill. As if I've got to start all over again, as many times over as the amount of people I see.

"I'll be starting school at the end of this month. And Will hasn't come up with the money yet. I'm getting very nervous." He looks annoyed. He seems to speak with the inflexibility of his anal rectitude. The preacher's voice is present.

"What does the racist think of that?" The first analytical move of the new season. We're both a little rusty.

"How do you mean?"

"The one who's disgusted with niggers."

Christopher blushes, caught. "They say: 'I could have told you those people are unreliable.' They sound very pleased." He grins. "They had expected it all along, but I had to be a sentimentalist to believe that blacks would come through."

"It supports the prejudice?"

"You bet."

△

"Will says the money will come soon. He's been saying that for two weeks now. School starts this week!" Christopher looks shaken and furious. Bigoted rage becomes irrepressible.

"We'll have to look for other sources," I say, contemplating whether I should pay for his classes myself. But I know that I can't. It would be too much.

△

"Will got me the money!" Christopher says incredulously as he walks in. He hadn't counted on it anymore. "I don't know if I'm happier with the money or with being able to trust Will again." He sits down in his chair in his maroon sweater carrying an armful of books. His spirit breathes excitement. And the T-cell count is up!

He loves his mind to be challenged again. "It makes me feel that I can go to the seminary. I'm sure I can do it." I feel the immense survival force, and silently bless Will for his kindness. "And I've decided to buy a funeral plot," he adds, practical as always. "I don't want to be a bother to anyone."

I marvel at his ability to lead two lives.

△

Not before October do dreams return to the surface. From the brown corduroy dream book.

Dream 31

I invite Mark to go for a ride in my car to his obvious delight. After riding around for a while I asked if he would like to get a burger and of course he was happy and said yes. After eating we stopped by the river and sat and talked. Mark seemed distant and hard to make feel comfortable: untrusting and on the defense.

It seems that Mark had left home because he felt it to be threatening and hostile. He sought safe haven in the church and his friend's houses but eventually emerged alone realizing that he was all he had. His life had been very provisional since making it as best he could.

When asked why he came to me he said because he needed me to love and nurture him and I needed him and that experience. He said I also needed someone to play with: no peer.

I asked him why he looked so lifeless and un-animated. He said he had known good people all his life but felt disappointed and let down because they hadn't helped him to feel safe and OK. Even with them he felt in danger and had to leave.

He said that his name really wasn't Mark but that he had tried to be my friend through Mark, but that I never made him feel seen and appreciated. When questioned further about his appearance he said that the way he appeared depended on the person that was looking at him. He had tried to show me that he looked like Billy, Mark and Laurence, but I always refused to believe him and reduced him to looking

*like he now appeared. Because of this constant
devaluing he had to keep his distance from me and
was only now trying to be my friend.*

"I see Mark on the porch of a house in the South
somewhere. I remember yellow pillars, and the house itself is
grayish. He's leaning against one of the pillars. One hand in
his pocket, tattered clothes, a waif like Oliver Twist....
Wait a minute, there had been something before that. I see
Mark on that porch. It's the Mark I know and love. He's
wearing a white shirt and jeans, like in the picture I have of
him."

He shows me a snapshot of a blond, short-haired young
man, mid-twenties, in a white tee shirt, looking up at the
camera with a shy but confident smile. He looks very open to
the photographer. The picture is taken from a height that
could be the level of a porch. I like Mark. I feel turned on.

"He's cute," I say.

"He's very attractive," Christopher confirms my response.
"Very slender and gentle. I loved him."

"So first you see Mark like he is in this picture, and then
something happens."

"When I come closer with my car, Mark has changed. I
don't notice him change. I still know he is Mark. He's about
the height of a twelve-year-old."

"Like Brendan with the punk haircut," I muse out loud.

"Yes, but Mark looks uncared for. Brendan's dressed punk
but dressed well—as far as you can say that of punk. Mark
looks disheveled and kind of exhausted. Withered. He's
standing by the pillar, waiting for something. I know that
he's Mark and I stop. I'm very happy to see him. He responds
like a frightened rabbit, cowering away from me. I ask him,
like you ask a frightened child, if he wants to come drive with
me in the convertible. He looks delighted. The next thing I
know we're driving in bright sunlight and Mark is enjoying
the ride. He's very distant toward me. Doesn't really answer
my questions. He mumbles and looks away from me, enjoy-

ing the wind from the green landscape in his face. He's also
feeling the leather on the seat. Mark has very sensuous hands.
I used to love the way he touched me...." Christopher trails
off.

"Then you get a burger?"

"Yes. We're driving into a place like McDonald's. We take
out two hamburgers and eat outside in the parking lot. I see
that Mark is enjoying himself. He's very hungry. I give him
part of my burger too. Then we drive off to the river. We sit
by the riverbank. We throw little stones in the water. The
river moves slowly. There we start our real conversation.
He's a little less scared of me. He still doesn't trust me, but
our relationship has improved since the ride."

"What's your conversation with him like?"

"What I wrote down is what I remember," he says,
pointing at the brown corduroy dream book on his lap. "After
I wrote it down, I thought that the beginning of the
conversation was about my own life," he adds, handing me
the book.

"'Home felt threatening and hostile,'" I read out loud.
"'Safe haven in the church and his friends houses'... 'alone,
realizing he was all he had. His life had been very provisional
since, making it as best as he could.'"

"Yes. But during the dream it was Mark's story, not mine,"
Christopher points out.

"Why Mark?" I ask.

"I loved Mark; he was beautiful. Now he's falling apart. I
don't know why Mark. Just that we had been very close. I've
only been that close with Laurence and Billy. But in the
dream we're so distant...."

"And he looked lifeless and unanimated."

"He felt unsafe, suspicious of people. So he stayed away
from them. He hid away, always leaving people, forced out by
a sense of danger," Christopher says with empathy. "That's
why he came to me. I had to nurture him, since no one else
would."

"And you need that experience because you have no peers,"

I summarize the brown corduroy dream book, open on my lap.

"I realized immediately that he was right," Christopher remarks, catching the drift. "Of course I have no peers."

"There are others with Aids," I insinuate, provoking an outburst.

"I don't want to be with other people who are sick! I just want to be with people who are in the heart of life. Not others around the edges. I get life from the living!"

This is his mantra, this "I get life from the living." It is spoken with overwhelming passion. The living are his angels of life.

"No, I have no peers. I'm all alone. And I need him."

I feel excluded. Though I am one of the living, I don't have Aids, which makes me not really his peer. Were I to have Aids, I wouldn't be one of the living. I feel lonely.

"I need him to play with," Christopher continues, oblivious to my presence. "He's like Marilyn, he wants to be touched. And he's like me, he wants to be seen."

"He's also like Peter behind you in the hospital bed, and like the young boy who jumps down into the chasm with you without a parachute. And like you being seen by the Spectre of Aids." I run rampant with associations. Christopher hears me. Suddenly we see each other. I feel my loneliness vanish.

△

"What was that stuff about him not really being Mark?" I ask.

"That was just like that insight about not wanting to be a woman but feeling the woman inside of me. He said that he was the spirit inside Mark and Billy and Laurence. At least, that's how I understand it now."

"And because you always saw him in others and never as a beautiful spirit of your own, he has withered," I conclude softly.

"I could never believe that I was beautiful, like Billy and Laurence. I still can't believe that. Mark is right. I still devalue him. Especially now, when I look at myself in the mirror and I see a skull for a face. Nothing about me is beautiful anymore. Thank God I don't have Kaposi's. I can't see anything beautiful in my face."

"You can't see the Billy in you," I say.

He grins, as if the idea itself is ridiculous.

"But this has been true long before you had Aids."

"Yes," he agrees. "Mark says that I haven't seen him for years. He says that he comes to me now to become my friend because I need him."

"You have to play with your spirit," I say, sounding a trifle stilted. It goes right by him.

"I love this dream," Christopher exclaims. "I feel it's important."

△

The next week Christopher comes in with a cold.

"Just a cold," he insists. We're both apprehensive.

From the brown corduroy dream book:

Dream 32

Dream of standing in crowd as if watching a marathon and two runners come in looking quite fatigued and disoriented. I guided them back through the crowd where they could be rejuvenated.

"You look very tired," I comment as he slumps in the rocking chair like a fountain gone dry.

"I've a transfusion coming up," he responds, takes out a tissue and extensively blows his nose.

"Do you think you're doing too much?" I ask, worried, referring to his schoolwork.

"I don't think so; I love school. It makes me think and question. I love the conversations I have with people these days," he says, for a short moment in high spirits; then he coughs. I'm not reassured.

"I bought myself a burial plot yesterday," he slips in a few moments later, sounding low. The contrast between his passion for life and his preparations for death boggles my mind. On the one hand he studies religion as if life were a vast plain ahead of him; on the other hand, he intends to sell his convertible to prepay for his funeral, so he won't be a burden to anyone. He's equally committed to a faith in life and statistical common sense about Aids. I realize that when I had suggested this to him, it had just been an idea for me. Seeing it being lived by Christopher moves me deeply. At the same time I notice my absolute certainty that he's not going to die. I feel more certain than ever. His doubts must be increasing. My certainty about his survival takes wings when his spirits fall into despair. *Christopher is not a statistic,* I hear me say inside myself. He's a potent spirit. I must somehow find an entry to his despair.

"I've been driving around looking at the change of the leaves. I love fall in New England," he changes the subject. "The colors are so intense. And it may be my last fall...."

"No, it won't," I interrupt.

He casts me a tired smile. "It may be my last fall," he repeats. "It's as if the trees radiate light from behind the leaves. Like translucent skin."

"Have you written lately?" I ask, noting his poetic mood.

"I haven't. Too much work for school."

"I'll be going home to Holland over Thanksgiving. I'm goint to talk to someone about the book we're writing together."

He looks unanimated. Usually, discussing the book we're going to write together picks up his spirits. We've had lively talks about the notes he's been keeping since late spring, though he never actually shows me any of his writing.

"You look like an exhausted long-distance runner," I call up the dream.

He sits listlessly.

"What's the finish line like?" I begin the reconstruction of the image.

He's resistant, preferring not to be bothered. But I don't seem to be able to leave him alone. I hope to lead him to the place of rejuvenation.

"There are stands. A lot of people. And those runners coming in, exhausted, crossing the finish line," he begins monotonously. "They're staggering. I catch them right after the finish line. One of them has his arm around my shoulder. He has no idea where he's going. The other one looks in a daze too. They're worn out to the bone."

"Try and feel how they're staggering and dazed. How they're disoriented for sheer exhaustion."

He closes his eyes.

I'm reminded of dream 7, dreamed just before the outbreak of pneumocystis last year, in which he's walking through his high school in a state of disorientation, unable to find his locker to get medicine.

"He's not steady on his feet," Christopher notes.

"Feel your feet," I reply, closing my eyes and feeling my feet.

"My legs are weak," Christopher says. "My head feels like when I can't find something. I seem to be losing things lately. I'm afraid my memory is going. They say that's part of Aids, going senile." He looks frightened.

One of the AIDS-related diseases produces dementia. I'm scared too.

"I do memory exercises," he says. "I'm scared of losing my mind. Then anything could happen. I wouldn't be able to take care of myself. That makes me frightened. Losing my mind would be the worst."

I can feel the disorientation of the long-distance runner at the finish line.

"I'm dizzy," he says after a few moments.

"You feel very weak, don't you?" I ask him, sad.

Christopher stares beyond me.

"Do you get to the place where they can receive care and be rejuvenated?" I ask him after a while.

"We're just going there when I wake up. I don't ever get to see it."

The promised land of rejuvenation.

▲

△

The transfusion revives him. Christopher goes out with his friends once again and studies with a passion. He says that he might want to become an analyst after doing his graduate degree in two or three years. I tell him that I'll do whatever I can to support him if he still wants to enter training when the time comes. Analytical training takes about seven post-graduate years. I'm thinking about his possible training without a doubt in my mind that he will live to complete it. I think in terms of ten years and don't even notice it.

△

From the brown corduroy dream book.

Dream 33

At some sort of school canteen watching out the back of the building where over the stadium is an airshow and fireworks. Later am at a kind of drug store. Sean is with me and this beautiful but small young man is trying on bathing suits and asking my advice of course to my delight. Sean makes a nasty suggestion about him and then is suggestive towards me which is a turn off. I'm turned on by the kid. Sean goes so far as to expose himself. I get up to see what a noise is out front with only a blanket wrapped around me. The police drive up and are after what sounds like my car. I remember I have parked it in someone else's drive down the street and forgot to move it. They are aiming to tow it. I try to stall them but have to run back home to get the keys. I don't know if they get the car or not.

We don't get to the opening scene of the dream. I can only speculate that the fireworks and the airshow seen from the back of the building, are related to a look back at the orgasmic beauty of the life force and the flight of high spirit. I believe (though I'm not certain) it was dreamed after the blood transfusion.

I instantly feel a physical attraction to the young man trying on the bathing suits in the drugstore. Not because I note in him the theme of rejuvenation inside the storehouse of medicine, but because of the effect he has on my genitals.

"You're in some kind of drugstore?" I ask.

"Yes. It's summer and I'm looking for something. I'm with Sean. He's someone I met here in Boston when I worked in fashion. I know very little about him."

"He acts a little like the salesman selling the pants off the young man in the department store."

Christopher understands my allusion and nods. "He's obnoxious. He just wants sex."

"And you don't?" I ask, neutral.

We smile at each other, glad to be together.

"But he's gross," Christopher clarifies. "He has no subtlety. I want to be close to that young man, not just have sex!" he concludes emphatically.

"What's the young man like?" I wonder out loud, feeling romantic.

"He's strong. He could be a dancer, but young. Puberty. Very delicate skin. Well proportioned but very small. Not small like Mark. But still small."

My arousal intensifies. My juices are flowing rapidly.

"He gets your juices going, doesn't he?" I remark. He's like the young man juicing up the aquarium.

Christopher's blush gives him away.

"What's it like when Sean exposes himself?"

"He does it surreptitiously, first to the boy; then he says something to me about the young man's buns. No one else in the store notices."

"How does the kid respond?"

"He doesn't quite know how to respond. I'm very turned on. I'd love to take him in my arms and just be with him. That's when I have to go and look at the noise out front."

"The police have come," I say. "Heat rises and the police are at the door to arrest your green Florida convertible." I'm quite pleased with my subtle implicit interpretation about how his exhibitionist fast-lane Florida heat gets stopped by the law, the superego. Christopher doesn't seem to notice either my interpretation or my smug pleasure.

"I was disgusted with Sean. I found his gesture repulsive."

"Hence the police," I insist.

Now he understands what I mean, but it doesn't really matter.

"Do you feel exposed in your blanket?" I ask after a silence during which he's waiting for me to ask him something.

"Yes. And I have to run home just dressed in a blanket, that's the worst of it. But I don't want them to tow my car. I'm very embarrassed." Paranoia zings through his voice.

"Feel the embarrassment," I say.

"I feel ridiculous. Everyone can see what kind of asshole I am."

"Literally?" I ask, mock-serious.

"I think the blanket covers me, if that's what you mean," he replies, not appreciating my pubescent humor.

"I'm just asking," I evade. "You're afraid what others would think of you. What do you feel people think of you in general?"

"I think they don't."

I stare at him, not understanding.

"People don't think of me. Some do, but I'm basically alone. If my roommate weren't there, I don't know what I'd do. I don't think anyone really cares about me."

"But you told me about your friends and how much they helped you."

"I'm alone."

"I'm here," I offer.

"Now you are, but not ten minutes from now."

I feel the guilt of not having more time to spend with him. And I feel my resistance, present from my very first telephone conversation with him, which makes me feel no desire to spend more time with him. We feel very separate. Christopher looks intensely alone.

13

On the cork board in my office hangs the program of studies at the C. G. Jung Institute of Boston where I teach my yearly fall course in dreams. This autumn it is about conflicting emotions; we study the nature of paradox.

Christopher has been very interested since the first moment I hung up the program in July. Now he's a vocal participant in the dream practicum and works well with live dream material brought in by other participants. He's usually among the last to stay, not so much to spend more time with me, but from a genuine interest in anything that is being discussed about dreams. He's very lively and I love having him there.

△

"What's a good book to read up on the history of psychoanalysis?" he asks me as he sits down in the rocker. He's carrying a book on psychology he had been reading out in the convertible across the street, enjoying the autumn sun.

I recommend my favorite book in that area. "But it has close to one thousand pages," I add. Christopher doesn't bat an eye. "I'll bring it for you next week," I offer. He's grateful.

△

From the brown corduroy dream book.

Dream 34

Dream of having a weasel who is like a pet. He likes to go across the street and play in the big fountain across the street. He wants to swim and frolic for a while and I let him. Then we have to go. I fear being bitten by him but am not.

"Do you cross the street together?" I ask.

"Yes, me and the weasel."

"He reminds me of the weasel man at the crossing of the waters," I remark. He hadn't thought of it and looks interested in the parallel.

"And?" he asks eagerly.

"Just that weasels and crossings seem to go together. And the god of crossings being Mercury, the thief in the night. Just that," I say, as deemphasized as possible. I've just finished the original Dutch version of my book *A Little Course in Dreams*, with an entire chapter on Mercury, so I feel like waxing eloquent. He's my dream practicum student and I'm his treacher (a typo I'll leave in; Mercury's treachery today is called Freudian slip).

But my desire for live material takes precedence.

"What does the fountain look like?" I ask instead of lecturing.

He looks disappointed about my changing the subject.

I compromise: "Mercury rules over times of transition, and his animal, the weasel, who actually likes to cross, is now not your adversary but your pet. He won't hurt you, and he loves the frolicky fountain on the other side."

"And what's on this side?" Christopher asks.

"I don't know." I reply both honestly and wanting him to ask himself.

Silence.

"How do you feel?" I ask.

"Mixed," he answers without further explanation.

"What's the street like on your side before you cross?"

"I don't remember. I can only see the fountain, and I feel the desire from the weasel to cross. I follow him. I remember that it is a relatively wide street. To some kind of park. The fountain is in some kind of park. I see some trees, but it's urban."

"You have no idea about the place before the crossing?"

"None."

"What is the fountain like?"

"It's a big stone fountain. Octagonal. A high spray of white water. My weasel loves swimming. It makes him lively. He loves to play in the shallow water and feel the drops rain down on him."

"Try and feel what your weasel feels like," I steer him.

"He looks like he's really enjoying himself. He's jumping around; splashing about. Totally involved. He loves it."

"Feel how much he loves it." I push.

"He loves to play. He just can't get enough. He's so lively. I love life! I love being alive!" He exclaims. His usually pale face looks flushed. I'm reminded of Mark, who came to play with Christopher.

△

From the brown corduroy dream book.

Dream 35

Dream seems to have lots of young men with long phalli. Three of them invite me to engage them in an underground room. There is a suggestion of S & M. more for effect than real.

He's been studying too much Jungian psychology, I think. Why else would he refer to *phallus* instead of *penis?* He prefers to see this image on a transcendental level: as symbolic intercourse with youthful spirits. The use of the word *phallus* annoys me. What's wrong with *cock*, anyway, I wonder rebelliously. Why do I feel so mean toward Christopher?

"I don't like real S and M," he begins without my prompting.

"What don't you like about it?" I ask. I'm all for it at this moment.

"I don't like pain," he says. My sadism disappears instantly. "I'm afraid of the pain like I had it when I couldn't breathe. It hurt so bad. Only morphine helped. I don't want that pain ever again." He looks afraid.

"You look scared," I comment.

"I don't want to think about it," he says with finality in his voice. His attitude conveys that I'd better not push.

"Are their phalli unnaturally large?" I ask.

"They're real big."

"Like Priapus?" I ask, referring to the nature god—friend of Pan the Goat—who's full of lust and is depicted as a walking erection. We had talked about him in class. Priapus loves lust; his sap is always rising.

"Same atmosphere."

"Seedy and alive," I remark. "Sado-masochism is like a game, like an aphrodisiac."

"Intensely sexual," he concurs.

"Juicy," I conclude, thinking of the sexual undercurrents. The torture and cruelty of underground sex are strangely exciting.

△

Around this time Christopher tells me a very important dream that he never gets to write down.

Dream 36

I'm in a garden, toward the back. The garden looks similar to the garden where the hippie woman gave me the mushy avocado resembling a bell pepper.

I'm the gardener. I'm pushing a flat wheelbarrow. On it are these red earthenware flowerpots upside down. I put the wheelbarrow down and stand up. I stretch my back and bend down again to pick up one of the flowerpots. Under it, staring at me, sits this little green frog man. He's green like a frog, glistening, but he's a little man.

I am the Lorax and I speak for the trees, Dr. Seuss's words echo through my head. The Lorax is the little vegetative spirit living in trees, who leaves the world when man kills the last of the Truffula trees, leaving nature a wasteland. The Lorax won't return unless new trees are planted. Why do I think of the Lorax right now? He doesn't look at all like this frog man. In my meanderings I almost lose the rest of the dream.

"He has fingers like E.T. and huge dark eyes like those tiny monkeys have. You know, the ones that look as if they're just eyes. He looks at me and I look at him. We keep looking into each other's eyes for a moment. Then he jumps off the wheelbarrow and scurries away into the woods."

Christopher digs into a plastic shopping bag and hands me a very clear painting in watercolors of a frog man, green, with long, thin limbs. You can see the moisture on his skin. His long E.T. fingers are spread wide. His eyes are deep brown. This is very different from Christopher's previous drawing of the scaly Spectre of Aids. But again it is the eyes that matter.

"I see him and he sees me. All that is happening is that we see each other. Then he turns around and runs off. I feel a pang."

"What kind of pang?"

"As if the plug's pulled. As if something is ripped out of me."

A moist vital organ was pulled out in the Marilyn dream.

"I see him scurrying away, and I feel that I've lost something. Something vitally important."

"What's it like to lose something vitally important?"

"Like you have to say goodbye to things. Everything you love is leaving you. Sometimes I feel so far away! So distant. Then I want to talk to people. And I miss my Christian community. I can't talk about religion with my friends. They're only marginally interested. It's not as vital for them as it is for me. It's not as important as their love life. Then I say: But it *is* your love life! And they don't understand me. I talk with my friend who gave me the job in the boutique. We talk about the pain of relationships. But sometimes I feel as if I'm miles away, even from him. John, my roommate, is falling in love with Eric and that's all he can talk about."

Christopher sounds annoyed the moment he talks about John. John has been his mainstay over the past year. John has had several involvements during this time, but Christopher has never minded them. But this sounds different.

"How serious do you believe John is about Eric?"

"That's not my business," Christopher says, irritated. "But they're always together," he adds in a catty tone. "They include me all right, but I feel left out. I think they're getting serious."

"And you don't like it."

"It's none of my business."

"Then why does it upset you so much?"

"I feel lonely. I'm full of self-pity." Self-hatred gushes forth.

"Are you afraid that John might leave you?"

"I don't think he will." I notice the hesitation in Christopher's voice. I feel alarmed.

"You don't sound sure," I observe gently.

"He's not going to leave," Christopher says, meaning *I don't want to talk about it.*

"Let's go back to the dream for a moment," I suggest. "Can you go back to the moment when you and the frog man are looking into each other's eyes?"

Christopher closes his eyes and concentrates.

"What is it like to be a little frog man like that?"

"He's very shy," Christopher tells me after a few moments. "He's very sensitive. He can feel exactly what I feel. His heart flutters. I don't want him to know me so well. But he knows me inside out. At first his knowing bothers me. But then he feels so familiar."

The alchemists called the helpful spirit *familiaris,* the familiar.

"What's his function?"

"He makes the plants grow. That's why he lives under the flowerpots. He makes everything green. That's why he is green. He's like a plant. His skin looks like chlorophyl. He's full of vitality."

"And what does he see when he looks at you?"

"A skeleton," Christopher mumbles, dejected.

"You don't look like a skeleton to me," I respond quickly.

"You're not a frog man," he retorts with a sad grin.

△

I wish I *were* that frog man, that vegetative spirit of rising sap whose chlorophyl transforms sunlight into life force. Without him Christopher is bone-dry and lifeless. I wish I *could* give him life. For the first time I doubt my certainty that Christopher will survive. But only for a short moment, then I'm sure again. We'll find the frog man again. We'll make him return. I'll be the skilled physician who can put the vital organ back in. We can make new Truffula trees grow from the single seed the Lorax has left behind. All it needs is the faith of a mustard seed.

I lend Christopher Dr. Seuss's hilariously illustrated children's book of rhymes about the Lorax. Christopher is amused, just as he was that time back in the spring when I suggested he drink tea with a Swiss extract of echinacea root to boost his immunity.

△

From the brown corduroy dream book.

Dream 37

In another dream am in a restaurant I really like. Seems to be out in the country outside Boston somewhere. I think how cozy it would be in winter at night with its fireplace and lots of windows to look out if it snowed. I am seated with 2 gay guys and am quite hungry. The food all looks good and is cheap. It seems to take a long time to get waited on. Waitress seems more fussing than helpful or suggestive. The seat I'm on makes for discomfort because it seems unstable or unlevel and is in fact resting in an irregularity in the floor. I'm having difficulty choosing something as if I can't comprehend the menu. There is a girl eating with us and marveling at the size and thickness of her bready tea she drops it on the floor.

"The waitress was terrible," he bitches. "I think service isn't what it used to be. In stores people are nasty to you. No sense of service left in some of these young people these days."

I hear his voice crackle with arthritis. "You sound like an eighty-year-old, Christopher. In an old age home they talk like that! Not that it's not true what you say, but it's the way you sound when you say it."

He looks perplexed and offended. I have raised the phantom of senility.

"I don't mean that you're literally an old man, but you're identified with Saturn." At the dream practicum we had talked about the god Saturn in his guise as the cranky old man who bitches about the young and lives in appalling isolation inside a stone house surrounded by lifeless rocks. There's no water for miles, no green as far as the eye can see. At these moments I believe that Christopher has aged fifty years in one year and that the moisture of life is evaporating. At such occasions I see his soul dry up before my very eyes. It puts all the juicy images in paradoxical relief. He looks pale and slight, but not skeletal.

"It scared me that I couldn't comprehend the menu. As if my mind is going." He's frightened. I feel stupid, stumbling into profound fear with heavy boots on. We're inches away from terror.

"Do you feel this equally strongly in your day-to-day life?" I ask.

"Not as strongly as when I reflected on the dream myself. That part of the dream really frightened me." I'm relieved that he had already gone in this direction himself. "Now you want me to really feel it, don't you?" he asks with biting sarcasm.

What a cruel labor analysis is. It demands feeling each emotion as deeply and as precisely as possible, thereby building the interior pressure to the critical point where the transformative chain reaction might take place.

"No," I lie.

"Good, because I wasn't going to," he exclaims defiantly.

"It occurs to me that there is a lot of food in your dreams," I open up another topic.

14

November. The landscape is stark. Bare trees. The real cold
has begun.

"I've been going to bars a lot lately. I've got to watch it or
I'll wear myself out. I'm drinking too much. They keep telling
me at the hospital that I shouldn't. But when I sit at the bar, I
want my beer. It makes me feel a little more at ease. Yes, I
know getting high isn't good for me. I had a dream even I
understand.

Dream 38

*We're at this swimming pool. There's a woman
on a raft in the middle of the pool with a drink in her
hand. She turns over on the raft and falls into the
pool, drink and all.*

"You get it? She fell into the drink."
I grin. "Are you going to stop drinking?"
"I try. But I do like an occasional beer."
"Occasional?"
"Lots of occasions," he quips.
"I'm not going to hound you. I leave that to the doctors.
Just watch out that you don't fall into the drink too deeply."
"Why are you always so fussy?" he jokes lightheartedly. I
can feel he's worried.

△

"I seem to be dreaming about water a lot," he begins,
puzzled. "I've had two dreams in a row with polluted water."
The dreams must bother him; he sounds apprehensive and
begins to tell them without prompting. "The first one I didn't

write down, 'cause I didn't get a chance. The other one I wrote down."

Dream 39

I'm on a boat, a speedboat. I'm with my friend. We're going very fast. The water of the lake is mucky. We are close to the dam. It is concrete and manmade, and it prevents the water of the lake from running out. At that point the water is most dirty. That's when we turn around and go back.

Christopher pauses. "I did some work on it myself," he continues. "What came to mind when I was thinking about the dam was AZT. It helps to dam up the hole in my immune system, and it pollutes me at the same time." He looks at me with expectation, to see if I concur. I'm impressed, even though he gives his interpretation without any feeling.

"Sounds true to me," I salute his insight. "Could you feel it when you thought about the image?"

"How do you mean?"

"Could you feel how you'd run dry unless you poison yourself?"

Christopher hesitates. "Probably not," he admits.

"What's the lake like? Is it big, small—what size about?"

"It's a large lake. We're in some cove or baylike area. The wind has swept all the pollution in that direction. It's a vile green slick," he says, repulsed. I feel a beginning of nausea weaken me.

"Can you describe the slick some more?" I request, feeling increasingly faint. Soon I will turn pale.

"It's slimy and thick."

"Like puke?" I ask, trying to get rid of my seasickness.

"No. Like an organic oil slick. Viperous green. Rot."

"Does it stink?"

"I don't remember a smell. I remember almost getting stuck in the slick. That was a frightening moment. I don't know who my friend was, but he was scared that it would get into the propeller and we'd be helplessly floating around in this muck."

"What's it like to get stuck in the muck?" I ask, nursing the faintness in my stomach.

"You'd become part of it somehow. Part of the muck. I was very scared."

"Feel the fear," I direct him.

Christopher concentrates. "I'm afraid I'll drown in it. The boat will sink eventually and I will drown in this icky green stuff. I can feel myself drowning."

"At what point?"

"When the motor stops and when my friend says that the propeller might be stuck. Then I get this sinking feeling."

"What's it like?" I ask, slowly recuperating as Christopher moves closer to the faintness.

"I can't breathe. It feels like in the hospital when I can't breathe. My lungs are drowning. I get so scared!" he exclaims suddenly, breathless with dread.

"And then your friend gets the motor started again and you get away," I can't help saying, no longer able to tolerate the suffocation.

Christopher's breath returns with a barely audible gasp. I sigh.

△

The second water dream, from the brown corduroy dream book.

Dream 40

Conversing with a beautiful woman from my house boat to hers. She has attendants like royalty and they are dressed romanishly. The water between us is icky.

"Is she like the queen who was coronated last fall?" I begin. (I've been going over his dreams in preparation for my workshop in Amsterdam. A few sessions ago I had asked him for free access to any material of his life that I needed to present his dreams at my Amsterdam dream practicum. "If

▲

anyone can be helped or can learn something from my life
and dreams, please use any material you need," he had
repeated to me emphatically, standing slightly bent in my
little hallway leading to the stairs down to street level.)

"Very different. This was Roman royalty. Like from
Roman times."

"Antiquity. Feeling more ancient?"

"Much more ancient."

"How do you converse?"

"We speak English together. But that doesn't make a
difference. She's Roman. She has a white toga. Long black
curly hair. Some of her attendants are blond. But I'm in a
conversation just with her. I think she's beautiful. We're
friendly. We seem to just have met talking across the water.
But I can't get to her. The water between us is too icky. It's a
barrier between her and me."

"Same muck as before?"

"No, brown. More like feces."

"Separated by shit," I conclude. Christopher grins.

"Smells?"

"Not that I remember," he remarks.

"What's your houseboat like?"

He hesitates. "I have a better image of hers."

"Go ahead," I encourage, attracted to the Roman lady.

"It's kind of square with a large deck all around it. She's on
the deck in the back. It's kind of luxurious. White. Mine isn't;
that I'm sure of. She's surrounded by her attendants. She's
looking straight at me."

"What kind of look?"

"Friendly, benevolent. She looks noble. Her eyes look
refined. Very dark. I like her. I would like to go over to her,
but that doesn't seem to be an option at this moment. She
looks very exotic. I like to talk to her. I could talk to her for
hours. It's kind of exciting."

"Does she get you excited?" I ask, feeling my own sexual
excitement toward the exotic princess.

"No. No, I don't feel any physical attraction toward her,

142

but I'm very curious," he says, obviously speaking the truth. I'm glad I checked to find out whether I was dealing with my own horniness or with his. My romantic excitement doesn't change by hearing his reply. I feel separate from him: me with my romance, Christopher with his feelings of curiosity.

"The muck separates you?" I ask, unconsciously alluding to my feelings of separation.

"It makes it so that I can't get to her physically. But we can talk together."

"Do you talk to her for a long time?"

"I wake up in the middle of our conversation."

"Can you concentrate on the muck between you that physically separates you?" I ask.

"It's brown. Filthy. Rotten. Putrid." He grins. "You want more? It's yucky. It's—"

"All right, I get the point," I smile, noting the way he humors himself away from the sense of rot. "Do you ever feel putrid?" I ask bluntly, aghast at my insensitivity.

"I often feel rotten, if that's what you mean," he replies, suspicious.

I don't say anything.

"You mean if I ever feel as if I'm rotting inside?" he asks.

I nod, holding my breath.

"Never!" he grins with acid irony.

I breathe and break out laughing.

△

From the brown corduroy dream book.

Dream 41

Walking down condo like stairs a godlike young man stands up on a scaffolding as though working. He has work boots and pants and no shirt and I later recognize him to be Lars in the soap opera.

"Who's Lars?"

"He's on my favorite soap. *Days of Our Lives.* I seem to be watching a lot of soaps," he ponders, then dismisses his observation about the amount of time he spends in front of the tube. "Lars is a Russian dancer who has defected. He's absolutely gorgeous. Like my friend from the blue jeans ads in Florida. I'm wildly attracted to him. He stands there with a sunny laziness. His movements are slow. I wish I could jump right onto the scaffolding."

"And make love with him right there," I add, certain that this time it is *his* arousal that stimulates my own lewd fantasies about Lars.

"I'd love to. But there is something unearthly about him. As if he's larger than life. Or more real than life, or something. Hard to describe. That's why I wrote 'godlike.'"

"Try to describe it," I insist.

"His muscles are perfect. He's perfect. He's built. Strong like Billy. His movements are very gracious. He's a wonderful dancer. His hair is dark and long. Feathered, shoulder length. He stands on the scaffolding like Michelangelo's David. Very seductive, languid. In the soap he always wears this skin-tight Spandex. I love his buns."

I almost salivate at Christopher's description. It is as if he's describing some delicious delicacy. Lars's exquisiteness rivets my desire.

"He's unbelievably attractive," I venture.

Christopher nods. "And he will never grow old, like the statue of David. He has something eternal about him."

"Eternal youth," I conclude.

"I want him so bad!" Christopher mutters, all steamed up.

We share an instant of passionate longing for this god of youth.

△

From the brown corduroy dream book.

Dream 42

I dream of eating a pomegranate.

"Just me eating the pomegranate. No location, nothing.

I've never eaten a pomegranate before. It has a hard rind. I don't even know how you eat one. How do you eat a pomegranate?"

"You eat the seeds; red seeds inside the fruit."

He nods, no longer interested in this incomprehensible sliver of a dream.

I'm struck by the image. It immediately reminds me of the story of the young girl Kore in Greek mythology, daughter of the wheat goddess Demeter, who was ravished and taken down to the underworld by the god of death, Hades. Down in the depths he gave her a pomegranate to eat. It is the fruit of the underworld, and those who eat it have to stay down there forever. That's how Kore became Persephone, goddess of death. The myth is widely known and central to Greek mythology.

"Do you know the myth of the rape of Kore?" I ask him.

"No."

"Hades, the god of death, took her down."

"You mean the queen of the underworld? I know that myth. We talked about it in my Houston dream group."

"Did you know that a pomegranate plays an essential role in that story?"

"Doesn't ring a bell. Tell me."

I begin slowly, measuring my words carefully. "After Demeter had saved her daughter from the hands of death, the first thing the mother asked her daughter was whether she had eaten from the pomegranate. Kore—which means 'young girl' in Greek—answered that she had only swallowed one seed. Demeter was heartbroken and said that in that case Kore must forever return to the underworld for part of the year. That's what made her Persephone, queen of death. The pomegranate is the fruit that makes you have to stay in the underworld. It makes death permanent."

"I remember," Christopher replies softly. "Do you think the Roman queen was her?" he asks after a while.

"I have no idea," I answer honestly. "The images of rot are striking though. Rot and underworld belong together." I

145

fervently hope that we don't have to go into the feelings behind the pomegranate and the permanence of death. I'm leaving for Holland in two weeks, and I don't want all that morbid material stirred. As if death weren't present to Christopher all the time. I'm resistant as hell. My fear of death must be close. I can almost hear its silence.

"Death doesn't frighten me that much. Eternal damnation does. It makes me feel horribly lonely. It frightens me that God will reject me for all eternity. It's like dying forever and never reaching death. Never finding peace. It makes me feel hollow and crushed. That's when I go to the bar to have people around. And that's when I drink. Especially now that John is away so often to be with Eric."

"You feel lonely," I say softly to no one in particular.

"Death is very lonely. It's like being deserted." He looks dejected.

Being deserted by life. That's why Christopher always says *I get life from the living.*

"Are you afraid that John will leave?" I reiterate the question I had asked him before. Christopher's roommate is the main "family" relationship he has at this moment in life. John is like a dependable brother.

"No" is again his answer.

△

It is two weeks before Thanksgiving at the session-before-last of my dream practicum at the Jung Institute in Boston. I'll be teaching in Amsterdam in two weeks and have typed out most of Christopher's dreams. When I gave him a copy, he looked very flattered.

The format of the practicum allows for one hour of work on alchemical material from Jung's incomprehensible masterpiece *Mysterium Coniunctionis* and one hour of work on material presented by a participant. We have just tortured our minds with intolerable paradox, and now it's time for a living dream.

"I had a dream last night," Christopher says to the group of

about thirty people. I'm alarmed and delighted. He looks pale
and set to present his dream. His cowboy boots are firmly
planted on the floor. We're sitting on chairs forming a circle
so that everyone can see everybody else. The group has tacitly
agreed that we're to work on his dream, and no one else
shows an intention to present material. We all look at
Christopher. He throws a quick glance into his brown
corduroy dream book.

Dream 43

*Dream of walking along a street of typical suburbia
—a beautiful sunny day about 1:00. My attention is
suddenly drawn to an odd vine or gourds growing on
one of the houses' mail box. The gourds, rather than
regular, are beautiful, opalescent, somewhat translucent glass like fine Christmas balls—large and
colored like gourds—green and yellow.*

*I am beginning to turn and leave when I look up
and see in the yard this very beautiful little child—a
girl. She is very bright and happy and cheerful and
friendly. As I start to leave I have the bad feeling that
she might walk out in the street and be harmed or
killed. I thought I'd play with her till someone
showed up. I beckoned to her and she readily came to
me and I picked her up.*

*I thought we could walk to the end of their part of
the walk and back. On the way back her mother came
out of the house and I explained what we'd been up
to. The little girl was having a big time and throwing
herself back. Because of an illness I have I feared
dropping the child but did not. I gave her to her
mother. She looked like a picture of summer with
whispy blond hair with barettes and a little sun suit
with one strap unbuttoned allowing the bib to flap.*

Christopher closes his eyes and begins to tell the dream in
a very plastic manner that transports us effortlessly into the
dream atmosphere.

▲

"What kind of street?" someone asks him after he's told us the dream twice.

"I'm walking down a street, and the houses around are clapboard houses. They're white and shiny. There are not many cars around, but some. Enough to make me be worried about the little girl."

"Are you walking fast or slow?" another participant asks.

"Not very quickly. I'm on a sidewalk. Down the street on my left I see the mailbox. Regular mailbox on a pole. I hardly notice it at first. But then I see these gourds. They hang like a vine off the mailbox."

"What are you feeling?" a question comes.

"I'm cheerful. It's a warm day. The sun is out. I've nothing else to do. Strolling along; very relaxed. Up. I don't feel like doing anything in particular." His friendly half-beak grin charms us all. His lower jaw is pulled to the right as he laughs. "I like summers here."

(During the following analytical hour when we work on the dream again, just the two of us, he adds: "People say that summers are muggy and hot here in Boston. But it's nothing compared to Houston. I like the summers in New England. I love the beaches. This summer I felt almost good.")

"What are the gourds like?" a man with a British accent asks. I like the different ways English can be pronounced. The British climate puts Christopher's sunny southern humor in a cool, airy perspective. Christopher thinks for a moment. "Are they as frail as I think they are?" the questioner clarifies.

"No, they only look frail. They're exquisite, but they don't seem particularly breakable to me."

The questioner does not look convinced. He still feels the intense frailty of the gourds. Several others concur. I feel the same.

"We may be hitting a resistance," I tell the class. "This may be a place to start digging. Tell me more about these opalescent gourds that look like Christmas balls," I direct Christopher. I try to forget all I know about Christopher's dreams of Christmas. It wouldn't be fair to the class to use privileged information. Then my work would look magical, which it shouldn't. Working with analysands in public is as fragile as the gourds in the dream. I don't want to suddenly fall deeply into an emotion that should emerge only in our intimate privacy, not in public. Especially when the image of fragility itself is concerned. Handle with care.

"Christmas balls remind me of my childhood. I was always very fond of Christmas."

"What were the Christmases in your childhood like?" asks a woman.

"We had real candles in the trees. It looked magical. I'd feel very much at home." I feel the preciousness of home as a safe place, a rare feeling in Christopher's nomadic life. I would ask further about the contrast between feeling like an animal hunted by illness and feeling Christmas, but I can't; it wouldn't follow from the material he's presented tonight. I wait for another member of the practicum to take the initiative.

"Did you have beautiful Christmas balls?" someone asks. I suddenly hear the word *balls* with a sexual ear, reminding me of Christopher's sexual vitality drying up. I think of the mushy avocado, looking like a bell pepper, which Christopher received as a medicine after the moist and supple vital organ had been removed. How much dry heat does it take to turn that moist vegetable into opalescent glass?

"Yes," he replies, "they were very precious to me. I still have some. In a box."

"Are they very breakable?" the man with the British accent brings in.

"Yes, they are. But I've moved around a lot, and I've never broken any."

(During the private hour following the practicum, he tells me how he's given a few of his Christmas ornaments to Laurence. It was the most precious thing he had to give. "I'm very happy that Laurence has some of them. It makes me feel closer to him, especially on Christmas."

"Are you going to use them again with John this

Christmas?" I ask him. Christopher's eyes shine.)

"What does it feel like to be breakable like that?" a woman asks kindly.

"It doesn't feel that breakable," he replies.

"That feels like the resistance again," someone comments. Nods left and right.

"Let's go elsewhere," I suggest. "What about the little girl? Tell us a little about her." I imagine a little girl in the exuberance of summer, the absolute overflowing joy of life. She reminds me of the flower girl of summer looking straight at me—her blond curls partially covering the bouquet of summer's abundance she holds in her arms—from the Art Nouveau poster of the four seasons we used to have on our bathroom door in Zurich. My kids were small then, my daughter about four years of age. "How old is she about?"

"I have a hard time judging the age of little kids," he says apologetically. "Four, five, maybe even three. Very little. That's why I'm worried when I suddenly see her running up to me in the street, cheering, happy—not at all concerned about the road. She probably didn't even know it was a road." I can see him see her behind his eyes.

"Describe her, please."

"She looks adorable in her little yellow sunsuit with the bib flapping. She makes me feel good. I tell her that we'll walk up and down their drive a little. She jumps into my arms."

"What does it feel like, holding her in your arms?" a woman's voice asks gently. I have my eyes closed and am concentrated mainly on atmosphere and tone of voice.

"I'm very happy. She is so trusting. She trusts me so totally; it makes me warm inside."

"And then her mother comes out," someone brings up too quickly, not giving the feeling of trust a chance to stabilize, a feeling that also pertains to the trust in the group. I immediately feel that we lose depth. I open my eyes, and so, a few seconds later, does Christopher.

"Don't go too quick," I warn. "Let's go back to where you have her in your arms." He nods. "Can you feel how trusting the little girl is?"

Christopher gets back into the trusting atmosphere.

"It makes me feel light. She jumps up and down," he replies.

Like a joyful young heart, I think. The heart of summer.

"She becomes real rowdy after her mother has come out," Christopher leads into the next scene himself. Now we can enter without losing depth.

"Is her mother upset?" I ask.

"No. I'm a little nervous because it looks strange, me with the child, and I don't want her to get worried and think wrong things. What matters most is the child in my arms. She's so full of life. She becomes so wild!"

"Can you feel that now?" I ask.

Christopher sits very still. I feel some people almost holding their breath. Suddenly he's crying softly. We look at him silently, watching him cry. I don't feel embarrassment in the group. The mutual trust holds.

"What's going on?" I almost whisper after a while.

"I was afraid that I wasn't going to hold her. She was becoming so rowdy, and I was beginning to feel weaker and weaker. I've this very bad disease, that makes me feel very weak at times, you know," he tells the class. "And she's so full of trust. I'm afraid I'll drop her and she'll fall to the ground. She has no idea of that. No inkling of danger. She trusts me totally. And then I can hold her. I don't drop her. It is such a relief. I feel so relieved. That's when I started to cry. When I could hold her. When I didn't drop her."

The preciousness and fragility of life are palpably present in the room, like translucent, filmy-thin Christmas ornaments.

15

At my dream practicum in Amsterdam we spend the better part of the weekend on Christopher's dreams. It gives me the opportunity once more to reflect on Christopher and to get responses from sensitive people. Everyone is moved by Christopher's courage. The group spontaneously calls him Frog Man after I've shown them the watercolor portrait Christopher made of the little fellow under the flowerpot. A card addressed to Frog Man, signed by most participants, is sent to my office in Cambridge, expressing how moved people are with his struggle. Christopher later loves receiving the card, showing a green froglike creature on the back. Some psychotherapists think it inappropriate to send a card to a patient after a case presentation. Their reluctance reflects one side of my own inner struggle between restrained professional formality and immediate, personal human intimacy.

The meeting with my writer friend in Holland goes auspiciously. He's just visited the West Coast and has written about Aids. As we walk through one of the most colorful neighborhoods in Amsterdam, he listens with interest while I tell him details about Christopher's and my plan to write a book together. He wants to help and thinks it can be published in Dutch. I also promise a magazine editor that I'll write an article about Christopher's dreams for the publication's spring issue. I'm excited about the prospects when I return to Boston.

△

"Christopher is in the Lahey Clinic," John tells me when I call after Christopher doesn't show up for his appointment.

"He's had another bout of pneumocystis." I feel betrayed by fate and dumbstruck. I had honestly thought that we wouldn't have to go through this again, that Christopher would slowly be doing better, that our work and his high spirits would protect him. And now Christopher might die; he might actually die! I call the number John has given me.

"Hello, Robert Bosnak," Christopher drawls nasally the moment he hears my voice. "I can't talk much." I can hear the effect of the plastic tubes going into his face, making speech cumbersome and twisted. "I have a beautiful private room," he adds. "They're taking great care of me. I'll be out in a week, they say. It wasn't as bad as last time. We caught it earlier. Didn't deny as long as last year." I imagine his grin as he's trying to comfort me.

The Lahey Clinic is close to my home. "Do you want me to come?" I ask.

"I'll come to you. I prefer that." He's trying to keep the analytical ritual intact. It makes him feel less sick, he explains to me later, to see my face in my office. My presence in the hospital would have made his sickness too real.

The first attack of pneumocystis took place when he was fired. Now it comes at the time that I've crossed to the other side of the Atlantic. The certainty that once convinced me I could save him now makes me feel guilty: guilty for my absence, guilty for the life I lead. Even though I can see that the guilt is the flip side of my magic wand that was to heal Christopher, my remorse doesn't lessen. It is apparently easier for me to chide myself than to feel my torn anguish about losing him.

△

I see him little more than a week later. He doesn't look as diminished as he did after his first attack. In fact, he sounds pleased about the way he has weathered this storm.

"When my cold got worse I went to the hospital right away. They kept me there, and the full blast of the pneumocystis came a few days later. But I was in intensive care already, so they could stay ahead of it this time."

"Do you remember anything from the time when it was at its worst?" I ask, noting that he wants to talk about his stay in the hospital and recalling the importance of the Marilyn dream the last time.

"I remember two things. Or it was one related experience. I died twice in one day." His voice is simultaneously worn and eager. "I'm not sure what came first. I woke up and I felt completely abandoned. I was terrified by the loneliness. I thought I was in hell. So I crawled out of bed and across the floor to the door and opened it. Then I yelled into the hall for someone to come. But everyone seemed like mechanical dolls—robots, empty shells. They came and put me back in bed, but even the nurse who had sat with me for a long time and who I liked a lot seemed as if she wasn't there at all. I felt so completely empty that I realized that I had died and was only a corpse. My life had been as meaningless as my death." He pauses.

"Then I woke up in the most perfect bliss. I felt accepted by God. I could hear God call my name. He kept repeating my name. And I knew I was dead and I had been forgiven. I don't know which experience came first. What struck me most, afterward, is how different they were, these two experiences. I've tried, but I'm not able to get back into them," he preempts any of my probing.

I'm happy to see him again. I've missed his crooked smile, and I realized that I'd already felt him to be dead.

"You don't look much worse than ever," I joke lightly. His eyes twinkle.

"Maybe these attacks will get shorter and shorter, and you'll be able to handle them better each time," I venture. Optimism takes hold of me again.

"I feel better than I felt before you left," he answers, carefully buoyant.

△

Christopher tells me the following dream.

Dream 44

I'm in a room on a bed. I'm naked. On top of me sits a young girl, slender and light. She's riding me like a horse. My penis is inside her. And with each gallop I feel more and more alive.

The life force seems to be pumping back into him. "You're being juiced up again," I notice. "Just like after your first attack. With the boy in the aquarium." Christopher looks mildly interested. It is becoming clear that he's losing interest in his dreams. He no longer writes them down and over the next two months reports only one other dream. Something else is weighing on his mind.

"Why a girl now?" I wonder out loud, feeling no energy in my question.

He shrugs his shoulders. The dream slides off his back. I feel alone with his dream.

"What's going on?" I ask.

"What do you mean, what's going on?" he scoffs. "I have Aids, don't I?"

"But you're also upset about something else."

"John said that he might move in with Eric," he bursts out.

"He tells you that now, not even a month after you get out of intensive care?" I ask, incredulous.

"It won't be the last time I'm in intensive care," Christopher replies, dejected. "He can't sit around and wait for me to get all better. He'd never move anywhere." Christopher takes John's side the minute he hears me being appalled at John's behavior. I'm furious with John. I can't believe it! This breaks all the trust Christopher has in life. This will sap his spirits. John becomes the immediate target for my rage at fate.

"Aren't you angry with him?" I ask the way I'd asked him about being kicked out of the seminary.

Christopher looks slouched like the zebra.

△

I write to the magazine editor in Holland that I have to

delay writing the article since new material indicates that we might be dealing with dream cycles, possibly demonstrated by a new dream Christopher has just had that looks very much like a dream from the beginning of the previous cycle of recovery after pneumocystis (dream 16). Christopher is again being juiced up after a debilitating crisis.

△

Christopher is carrying my thousand-page book on the history of psychoanalysis. He puts it on the low round table beside us. "I don't feel like reading heavy stuff right now," he explains.

"What about school?" I ask.

"I don't feel like going," he answers.

"Then what about your plans?"

"Like going to the seminary and so on?" he asks.

"For instance."

"Robert," he says, serious with friendly humor, "you know the statistics. Do you really think I'm the only one who's not going to die from this?"

We look at each other, and we both know that he will die of Aids. The clutches of optimism dissolve, and we see what lies ahead. We're very close.

"Not that I'm not going to fight for every minute," he utters, more strongly. "I'm going to outlive the statistics. Live another two years, maybe."

△

"I have to start looking for a new roommate," he tells me one cold January day. "John is moving out in March."

I am shaken. I must have believed that John was not going to go ahead with his plans of leaving Christopher behind in such a frail condition. I had traced the extent of my anger at John to my own discomfort about having to leave Christopher again and again. I'll have to teach in Amsterdam once more in February. John was important to have around. I feel the full burden of Christopher's motto, "I get life from the living." The resistance I had from the first time I heard his voice on my answering machine returns momentarily. I want to drop him like a hot potato.

"Are you sure?"

"He said so. He and Eric told me together when we were at Eric's house last night." Christopher looks gray; his clothes are dark. "I'm going to put ads in the paper for a roommate tomorrow."

"Will you tell them you've got Aids?" I ask, wondering if I would move in with a man with Aids.

"Of course," he responds without hesitation.

I wouldn't move in with him, I realize. I hate Aids. I feel John's betrayal as my own.

△

"My friends can't believe that John's actually moving out," Christopher tells me. He's put ads in the papers and is waiting for answers. "People will come," he says, stretching his confidence to cover his despair. "I didn't know I could have so many friends," he adds. "Everyone comes to talk with me. I feel like a therapist. I hear so many stories. But I get tired of having to defend John to all my friends. I keep telling them that John has a right to move in with Eric. They love each other, and they should be living together. I feel like a fifth wheel anyway."

Christopher's nobility strains my ear. "Do you really believe that John is behaving all right?" I ask.

"Yes," he answers adamantly. I don't believe him; maybe because he is kidding himself or maybe because I despise my own inner John.

"I had a dream," he says.

Dream 45

I'm in my convertible driving down to the river. There's a party down by the river. Lots of people are milling about. The atmosphere is busy and fun. I walk into the crowd. But it is as if no one is noticing me. I am completely on my own, walking through a crowd of people who don't seem to see me. I feel isolated. Then I see in the mud a tiny little gold coin. I pick it up. It is extremely precious and has triangles on it. Triangles within triangles.

"Could you draw those triangles?" I ask.
Christopher nods. "I will."
"You feel isolated in the crowd?"
He stares down. I don't push any further.

△

The session after the river-party dream Christopher gives me a large pencil drawing of a circle. The circle is horizontally divided by about six parallel lines, each forming the base of a downward-pointing triangle.

"This side's up," Christopher tells me as he places it between us, making sure I see the triangles pointing down.

"What do you make of it?" he asks.

I have no idea what to reply. Only one association keeps coming to mind, but I don't know whether it has anything to do with Christopher or it is purely my own paranoia. Christopher is waiting for me to say something. I want to say something. But I don't know whether I should.

"The only thing that comes to my mind is the pink triangles gays had to wear in concentration camps," I hear myself say. I have never told him I'm a Jew. It feels important that I be his brother in Christ. He doesn't know that my nightmares are of concentration camps I have never been in but in dreams.

"I hadn't thought of it," he remarks, contemplating my association. Though sounding familiar, it doesn't seem to move anything in him. We must be in different worlds.

"Do you feel isolated in the crowd?" I repeat my question from the previous hour. He doesn't hear me.

"The most striking thing about the coin is its value. It's precious like an antique coin. It is tiny, tiny."

Like a little girl in a yellow sunsuit. A tiny drop of life, precious like a Christmas ball.

"Can you feel just how precious?"

"No," Christopher replies, tired of feeling things. He leaves me behind in his dreamworld. I see him in the hall of the hospital, screaming for doctors and nurses and finding only robots.

"Tomorrow the first man who answered my ad will come to see the apartment," Christopher says, tense. He looks so alone.

△

He puts the two pullover sweaters and a cardigan on the little table between us. "Which one do you want?" he asks. "I'm cleaning out my closets, giving everything away I don't need. These are my favorite sweaters. I've hardly worn them. Which one do you want?"

I am moved and pick the dark maroon cardigan.

"Good choice," he compliments me with the experienced voice of the fashion professional. "Some of my friends will be very sorry. I told them you had first choice."

I'm flattered. At the same time I wonder if I will ever wear the cardigan or if I will fear wearing his skin.

"I had it dry-cleaned," he tells me as he folds it and hands it to me. I shake his hand, then hug him. I'm scared of Aids. I can hardly feel Christopher. Am I a member of the fun-filled party by the river, blind to Christopher's presence? Have I left him too, so I won't get hurt, like John?

"I've had three people look at my apartment, and two want to live with me," he says, relieved. "I liked both of them right away. Now I have to choose. I'm really happy that people still want to live with me, even with Aids. People seem to like me!" Christopher looks pleased for the first time since John's announcement.

"One day you don't know who you're going to live with, and the next day you have to choose. I don't like to choose. I like both of them. Maybe if I tell you about them it would help. One is very handsome. He's outgoing and a lot of fun. We were talking for hours. He likes to go to bars. I felt very alive with him. He really made me feel good. The other is kind of quiet. He says that he likes to stay home a lot at night. He doesn't turn me on, but that may be good for a roommate. He feels very reliable to me. And supportive. I'm afraid that the handsome guy will never be home. Then I might as well be alone. I have that now when John is over at Eric's all the time. I know who I should choose. I can't choose my roommate on the basis of how turned on I get. I'd love to be with that handsome man, but I don't know if he'd be there for me when I'm sick. Then again, we had such a wonderful talk. That does me a world of good. It makes me realize how I've changed. I don't feel like going out. Even if I'd have the energy. The first guy has money, too. He could buy us a fridge. John is taking the fridge, so I'll need one."

"I have an old fridge in my barn," I say. "You can have it." I know that I want him to be with the reliable man who will be there for him.

"At least I know who you want me to choose."

"Don't we agree?"

"We do. I'll ask a friend with a van to pick up your refrigerator. Thank you."

"I also think you should have your dream book and the pictures of the frog man and of the Marilyn dream," I remark. Christopher nods, not particularly interested. I go over to my file and take out his material. It is part of him, and he should hold on to it, I believe. He had given me his dream journal to copy for my work on our book. He isn't working on it anymore. I hope to rekindle his interest by returning the pictures he had painted.

While copying his dream book I discovered a dream I have never seen. It is written on a loose leaf. He tells me that it is from last fall when I was in Holland, just before he went to the hospital. I ask him for associations. Christopher is apathetic.

▲

△

Just before I leave for Amsterdam again I call Christopher's doctor. He tells me that Christopher is living purely on his will to survive. The fact that he is still alive is a tribute to his spirit, says the doctor. I'm upset that my Amsterdam spring workshop had to move to February this year. I hate to leave him now.

"I'll be all right," he soothes me. "I've got this move coming up. Plenty of work to do. My new roommate is great, and John is helping me with everything. I know John's my friend. He'll always be my friend. He said that he'll probably see me more often when he's living with Eric than he has seen me lately. I don't feel angry toward him anymore." Christopher sounds simple and genuine. I feel relieved and absolved by proxy.

"In May I'm going to Houston again. Maybe I'll stay this time. Maggie and Laurence called me. They want me to come. I said I'd come in May because that gives me time to move in. I'm looking forward to Houston. I could use some warm weather. I'm cold all the time."

16

When I return from Holland on February 23 I have a message from John on my machine that Christopher is in Mass General again. Pneumocystis. Intensive Care.

I go to see Christopher after work. There is no doubt in my mind that now I have to see him in the hospital. John's message has a ring of finality to it. I feel surprisingly little as I try to find a space in the parking garage of the hospital. The garage sounds hollow. The sound of my driving is reflected back to me. I feel nothing. Then I'm annoyed that I'll be home late tonight. Jet lag is still pulling me down. I shouldn't work right after coming back from Europe, I tell myself. I look at my watch. It is two A.M. Dutch time. Shit!

I wander through the fluorescent halls of disinfection, asking people where to find the Bigelow building. A very gentle man at the desk of the I.C.U. tells me to wait a moment. It is past visiting hours. I tell him I'm Christopher's analyst and that I have just returned from a trip abroad. The man becomes extremely helpful. "I'll see if the nurses are working with him. You may stay as long as you like." He walks down the corridor and turns right at the end. After a few minutes he comes back. "They're just changing his bed. They'd prefer if you'd wait a few minutes."

I lean against the glass door, looking around, making mental notes for an I.C.U. scene in a novel I am writing. I feel like a detached eye and remember Claude Monet chiding himself for his cold eyes, enabling him to paint the dying of his beloved wife.

I'm called in by a nurse who is as friendly as the receptionist. The atmosphere is quietly efficient. The nurses live in a brightly lit glass hut, and all around machines are giving life to people. Christopher is in the corner room. I am asked to wash my hands carefully and then put on plastic gloves. As I wash my hands I see machines. Beige machines, silver machines, machines on wheels, machines on stands. Bottles feeding from everywhere into his arms. Everything is pale: the machines, the bed sheets, and Christopher's skin. His beak is more pronounced than usual. He looks like a geriatric patient I once had in a mental hospital, ninety-eight years old, smearing his feces all over the wall. And I had to clean it up. Out the window, the head beams of tiny cars stream silently by. The rain makes Boston glisten. Then I realize that I don't want to see Christopher. I am in the claws of an overpowering resistance against feeling. I breathe deeply and see his face.

His eyes are bright, and he is very happy to see me. He lifts his arm to greet me, but it is tied to the bed, so it looks like an ineffectual gesture. I fall into his eyes. In one surge all my feeling for him resurfaces, and I begin to cry behind a disintegrating mask of initial good cheer. I walk over to him and hold his bound hand between my hands. It is cold: my hands are colder. He makes a face around the tubes through his nose and mouth, disapproving of the coldness of my hands. The expression has an undertone of a worried mother, wanting me to take good care of myself.

"It is blistering cold out," I reply to his gesture. I feel some tears rolling down my cheek and see him notice them. I put my left hand on his forehead and stroke it. Our relationship has transformed. His skin feels soft like a baby's. A machine breathes for him. Nurses tell me later that he will go back to his own breathing soon. He's been on a respirator for over a week. The doctors had a conference with Christopher during which they asked him if they should go all the way and give him all available life support, or if they should slow down and let him die. Christopher had told them that they should try everything they could to keep him alive. "I don't want to die!" he kept repeating. He may die soon either way, the doctor told me. He's living entirely on his survival spirit now.

Christopher has become pure flame with hardly any fuel left as his body melts away like wax. It is the "running on empty" of his dreams.

He motions with his right hand as if he were writing. I give him my appointment booklet and a pink extra-thin felt-tip pen and untie his hand. I look at my hands and notice that I am not wearing the prescribed gloves. We are fused again.

At first he writes a capital *R*. It looks as if he wants to write a whole sentence, beginning with my name. Then he looks very tired and scribbles something without being able to look. I can't read his writing, which is a disappointment. His effort had been substantial. I take a sheet I find on the counter and write down the alphabet. I point out letters, and he nods when the appropriate one comes up: B-R-O-N-C-H-O-S-C-O-P-Y. I compare it with his scribble, and now I can just make it out.

"You just had a bronchoscopy?" I ask, wondering what they found when they sent their microsubmarines down his lungs.

Christopher nods.

"And you want to know the results?"

He nods again.

I leave him behind and walk to the door to get a nurse. Then I turn around. "You won't pull out the tubes while I'm gone?" I ask, motioning to his free hand. He waits for a comic moment of overacted hesitation, as if he were not quite sure whether or not he would disconnect himself from all the machines during my minute of absence. Then he has a mischievous smile on his face.

"It looks pretty bad," the nurse in charge of Christopher tells me after I have identified myself. "But he wants us to continue. I do know some men who have pulled through in this stage. They have one on the third floor now who was in the I.C.U. a few months ago. He was every bit as bad as Christopher. And he's pulling through this one...." Her voice trails off, as if she's thinking about the next bout for the man on the third floor. I think of Christopher's weasel man, who charges so much that Christopher may not have enough left for the next crossing. "But it is rare," the nurse adds honestly. "Christopher may not have more than a few weeks. The courage of these men is incredible."

"Does he get a lot of visitors?"

"All the time."

I go back in and pass the box of rubber gloves. I feel no desire to take a pair, even though my street germs may infect him. Touch is more important. Flesh on flesh.

He looks at me with intense expectation.

"People have pulled through worse crossings," I say.

He looks dissatisfied. He wants a precise answer.

"Pretty bad," I say. "You're going to need all your wits about you to pull through this one." He nods, ready for any kind of battle. My admiration for him is boundless. I put my cheek to his forehead.

△

The next day he looks even more tired than the day before. The nurse tells me that they had him off the respirator for a while, and breathing by himself is exhausting. I don't know what to say. We sit quietly for a few minutes. A single tear of Christopher's rolls down onto the sheet.

"You want me to tell you one of your dreams?" I ask suddenly, just to have something to monologue about.

He nods eagerly.

First I untie his hands, and then I begin talking about the weasel man, followed by the mushy avocado dream. It is like telling a child his favorite stories.

"I have looked at this dream from the fall again. The one we didn't get a chance to work on. It seems very important to me. I have it with me. Let me read it." I dig into my black bag, filled with the dreams of different patients. I'm transporting them from my office to my home.

From a loose leaf in the brown corduroy dream book.

Dream 46
Dream of going to Billy's folks' house—a big old

▲

house like theirs but not actually theirs. It turns out that they are moving and Billy has died of Aids. This makes me very sad and at two or three points I cry and express my grief. They seem to resent me doing this and I feel guilty for wanting to cry. Their appearances are altered. They seem gaunt, older, not very loving.

For some reason I feel funny about this thought I feel they would like me to leave. I go upstairs to Billy's room to see the body. I find Billy not dead, but ill. It's as though they had given up on him and he on himself and were waiting and wishing him dead. In fact the coffin—a cheap one considering their wealth —was in the house waiting for him.

He lay on his bed nude, though a little thinner, still very beautiful to me. I went over and sat beside him. He was laying with his legs protruded—Pietà like* I love him so much and I reach out and stroke his body touching and smoothing his skin which is more like mine than his.

I begin to reason with him that there is no reason he should give up and die right now. I ask him if there isn't anything he still wants to do. I have the definite feeling that I can cause him to change his mind and can love him back to life.

When I tell the others of the exchange they seem glad though less enthusiastic. I felt free to unite with (even physically) love, protect and defend Billy from the others.

After waking I sensed the message of Aids having come through Billy as symbol and those who worked against Him. Also was the knowing that I was somehow loving and nourishing a part of myself as indicated by the skin that I recognized.

---

*The Pietà is a sculpture by Michelangelo portraying the Virgin-Mother holding the dead Jesus on her lap after he is taken down from the cross.

Christopher has tears in his closed eyes. He seems to have reexperienced the dream and appears to sigh when I'm finished reading.

"I also found something else in your dream book." I dig into my black bag again and take out the photocopies of the brown corduroy dream book I had taken with me to Amsterdam. I roam through the papers. "I've never seen this before either. I noticed it when I was reading over your dream journal on the plane." He grins when he hears that I had been reading his dreams on the transatlantic crossing.

From the brown corduroy dream book.

Billy

—*source of strength*
—*beautiful, strong, accepting, male, related*
—*able to overcome intimidation of being related to otherness—the faggot*
—*Christ figure inside me, loving me, loving knowing me, relating to me, teaching me to love at least one faggot—me*

"You have learned to love yourself, mother yourself," I conclude.

Christopher has both eyes closed, far off in thoughts. I have to go home. I stroke his hand as I tie him back down to the bed.

Walking down the stairs of the hospital, I feel the preciousness of life pulse through me.

△

I no longer take the elevator. Walking up the stairs gives me a chance to prepare myself mentally for our meetings. Each day I push myself over to the hospital, not wanting to go. Then, as I get to the stairs, I can notice a sudden longing for him and I hurry. As one foot follows the other, I feel the contrast between my living and his dying. While washing my hands to greet him, I ponder the guilt feelings concentration camp survivors have toward their fellow inmates who didn't make it. Behind me I hear a nasal "Hello." He's off the respirator.

"I'm glad you can talk again," I reply, relieved.

"Laurence was here" is the first thing he tells me.

"When?"

"When I got ill," Christopher replies, deeply touched.

"He came up from Houston?" I ask the obvious.

He nods.

I feel no jealousy toward Laurence, even though it is the very first thing he wants me to know the moment he can talk again. I just feel gratitude and comradeship with Laurence.

"So many people came," he whispers, crying.

A nurse comes in to adjust one of the I.V.'s.

"They're taking good care of me," Christopher says when she leaves. "They don't spend as much time with me as at the Lahey Clinic, but they're kind." He looks tired after this long sentence. He shouldn't talk much.

"Shall I tell you some more dreams?"

"The one about Billy," he says, closing his eyes, exhausted. I'm telling my son a bedtime story. I shouldn't forget to buy him a teddy bear. I remember the dream of the cockscomb bracelet becoming a chain of teddy bears. I shouldn't forget to get him a teddy bear. I forget.

△

The friendly receptionist is on the phone and motions that I can just go in. When I enter, Christopher is half naked on the bed. He's on the respirator again. The nurses have just been washing him, and they must have gone somewhere to get something. His nightshirt is up over his waist. Catheters are coming out of his penis. Seeing me notice, he makes a motion with his index finger and his thumb, indicating something very small. I look again and see that his penis is almost entirely drawn into his body. It is tiny.

"Does it hurt?" I ask.

He shakes his head and intensifies the "small" gesture with his right hand.

"It has become so small?"

Christopher nods and grins with melancholy. I remember his pride in his large cockscomb. We love being men together.

△

It's been two weeks since my return. Christopher's health has been steadily improving. He's off the respirator for longer periods of time. My mood is hopeful. While I'm at the hospital, his friends from Houston call, and I tell them that he's doing much better. Optimism is sneaking back in.

I'm going in on Saturday morning. It's not my usual time. I have been going five days a week but not last weekend. Feeling an urge to see him, I drive to Boston from my home outside of the city.

When I come in he's frantic. I haven't seen him like this. The nurses have told me that he sometimes get extremely agitated. This is an animal in a deadly trap. He's terrified. He motions for the alphabet paper. And points out L - A - H - E - Y.

"You want to go to the Lahey Clinic?" I ask.

He points out T - H - E - Y - K - I - L - L.

"They're killing you here?"

He nods emphatically. The whole power of his conviction is in that one nod.

"But you can't just leave here. You're too weak."

Now he becomes aggravated and motions for pencil and paper. He writes in large letters, some written on top of the others: IT IS MY RIGHT!

He looks at me with the fury I have seen in the eyes of a stroke patient who's trying to make people understand him but nothing gets across.

"How do you want me to do that?" I ask, exasperated.

He breaks out in a broad smile. He points out the name of a doctor on the alphabet sheet.

"Was he your doctor at Lahey?" I've only spoken with his physician at Massachusetts General Hospital, a well-known authority in the field of AIDS medicine and a pioneer in the use of AZT, in whom Christopher has always had great confidence. Christopher went to Lahey last November because of its relatively pleasant rooms and service, but decided to return to his regular physician because of his skill and reputation.

Christopher nods.

"I'll think about it," I hedge.

Christopher looks outraged; fury contorts him.

"I'll call," I promise, overburdened.

Christopher looks relieved and closes his eyes, worn out.

"You want me to go?" I ask after a while.

He nods, almost imperceptibly.

"It is Saturday today. I will be back on Monday. I'm not coming tomorrow, you understand?" Same nod, but even fainter.

All of Saturday I am tormented over whether I should call this doctor at the Lahey Clinic. Christopher is so weak that a move would kill him. I know that. But it doesn't change the certainty I have that I must see to it that he gets moved. I've got to get him out of there. I imagine the scorn of the doctors when I approach them with the ridiculous idea that a patient in an almost terminal state should be moved to another hospital for no apparent medical reason.

I talk about it extensively with my wife, who listens but doesn't advise me. I pace the house, go to the video store, rent a silly teflon movie, and let the impending decision slip my mind until the next day.

Sunday is hardly different, with a pinch of added guilt that I haven't made up my mind. I'll call Monday. No reason to call over the weekend.

Monday night I go to Christopher.

"He's been hardly responding since this morning," the nurse says. "I think he's slipping into a coma."

"He's very weak?" I ask.

"Very."

I'm both heartbroken and relieved. The decision has been made for me.

"He asked me to have him moved to the Lahey Clinic on Saturday," I say.

"He wouldn't make it down to the ambulance," the nurse replies with a sad smile.

"I told him I would try," I add.

"You did what?" Her eyes are filled with humor.

"It calmed him down," I cover up, as if my belief in his conviction about the necessity of getting out of this place had been a ruse to soothe him.

"It certainly did that," said the nurse in amused admiration of my apparent psychological trick. "He's been much calmer since Saturday. I was on duty Saturday night, and he was very peaceful. But tonight I can't reach him. The day nurses said that they weren't able to all day."

Robert, get me out of here! I hear Christopher's voice in my head. *Out of this death trap.*

His face is still as wax. The machine breathes for him. I notice the plug of the respirator going into the socket. He gets his last juice from the wall.

I bend over by his ear and whisper, "Robert, Robert."

The faintest of smiles mists over his placid face for an instant.

I put my cheek against his. "You get life from the living; remember, life from the living," I whisper intensely.

Again a breeze of a smile blows over his face, the soft skin taut over his skull, making him look like someone with too much of a facelift.

Praying that he will take life force from me, I concentrate on giving it to him, my cheek pressed against his, his hand in mine.

No more responses. I sit down, close to his ear, and tell him the Billy dream.

△

By midweek he can't communicate back to me anymore. I just sit and tell dreams, remembering them as vividly as possible, whispering them in his ear, feeling very silly at the same time.

When I come in on Friday and whisper in his ear, I suddenly know that it is over. He's very distant, almost unreachable. I concentrate all the energy I have, letting it accumulate for as long as I can hold it. Then I whisper softly in his ear:

"Ethel loves you.

"Hank loves you.

"Maggie loves you.

"Laurence loves you.

"John loves you.

"Mark loves you."

Pause.

"Billy loves you." I hold my breath for a moment; then all my feeling for him flows into voice:

"And I love you."

I get up. My back aches from having bent over in an uncomfortable position for too long. I stretch and look at him again. Did I get through? I bend over once more and kiss his forehead.

And then I leave. It is very still in the stairwell of Massachusetts General Hospital.

△

Christopher died that night.

Epilogue

The night before writing down my memories of Christopher's death, memories I had postponed to the very end, I dream:

> I am in a camp of *Outward Bound*. We have to learn to go through dangerous terrain. I'm with my teenage son. I have to go down a very narrow rocky shute. I am terrified. The most terrifying thing I can think of is going down a very narrow shoot and getting stuck, like those children in Dickens's time who were sent up the chimney to clean it, only to find themselves getting stuck, never to move again. I stand in front of it and dare not go through it. Next to us, over on our left in the green grass among the rocks, there is another shute. This one is smaller and smoother. It is for children. My son looks sad. He says, "I live with others; dying I do alone." Then he goes down the shute.

Will does the funeral service. He pulls out all the stops, and we go back and forth between Heaven and Hell. I can make out some of the people I know from Christopher's stories. One man looks griefstricken. He's supported by another man. John and Eric. I go up to John and introduce myself. His pain is palpable. I relay a message Christopher had given me in the hospital one day that he could talk, saying that I should have his brown corduroy dream book and the drawings. I tell John I'll be in touch. I wait more than a year, and by then John has moved. I leave a message for him to call. He doesn't. The same resistance that made me postpone working with Christopher now gets transferred to the book I promised him I'd write.

△

For over nine months I was subliminally terrified that I'd die of Aids. Christopher was dead, but our fusion wasn't.

When I finally took the HIV test, I was consciously petrified for two weeks. I hadn't taken the test before, not only because of my fear, but also because of a strange loyalty to Christopher. As long as I was scared stiff, I was with him.

The test was negative.

△

We were going to write this book together, you and I. And we did.